in modern day Turkey, and ended up set[illegible] t is where Terah died. We find ou[illegible] ed a woman named Sarai [illegible] y lived in ancient Mesop[illegible] or so. An unremarkable [illegible] become very remarkable [illegible]

We do not know wher[illegible] start of Genesis 12 or what he was doing. [illegible] was out with his herds or resting in his tent, escaping the noonday sun. Perhaps he was at the marketplace, buying and selling animals or produce. We know little of his context, but we do know that into his ordinary life comes the Word of God. Without recorded pleasantries or introduction, the Lord taps him on the shoulder (as it were) and simply says: "Go from your country and your kindred and your father's house to the land that I will show you" (verse 1). *Leave your home and everything that is familiar, and go to a place that is yet unknown to you, a place that I will show you.* It is a challenging thing to ask of Abram, but that great call is immediately joined to an even greater promise:

> "And I will make of you a great nation, and I will bless you and make your name great, so that you will be a blessing. I will bless those who bless you, and him who dishonors you I will curse, and in you all the families of the earth shall be blessed" (verses 2–3).

It is a stunning promise. It is almost too much to contemplate that this childless man will father a nation. This unknown man will have a great name, and through him, blessing will come to others. It is a staggering prospect.

As we zoom out from Abram and read the wider story of the Bible, we soon see that the story points ultimately not to the arrival in the land or the multiplication of Abram's descendants. It points to one great descendent who would bring the blessing of God's salvation to the whole world. The greater Son of Abram will come and will live the perfect life and then die to bear the penalty for sin, so that all who come to him might be forgiven and enter the family of God. The curse will be lifted. That is where this is all heading. This is a *gospel* promise at the start of Genesis 12. In fact, the New Testament will teach us that it is *the* gospel promise. Abram is blessed with the blessings of salvation right here. He is promised a future, a homeland, and a great people. In Christ, we have that future, that promised homeland, and that great people with whom to share those blessings in eternity. In Abram, we have a picture and a foreshadowing of how God's salvation blessings can come to us.

God's blessings come by his initiative

The story of Abram teaches us that the salvation blessings of God come to us by his own initiative and grace. We learn very little about Abram in the verses leading up to the pronouncement of this great blessing. He was son of a man named Terah, married to a woman named Sarai, from a place called Ur. That is more or less it. We do not hear of Abram doing much in chapter 11, either good or bad. And then suddenly, out of nowhere it seems, comes one of the most monumental promises ever spoken by God anywhere in the Scriptures. It was not grounded in anything Abram had done or would do—but simply in the initiative of God himself. God has chosen Abram. He is going to bless him, make his name great, make him a blessing, and give him a whole nation's worth of grandchildren. God is going to do it all. Abram is little more than a bystander at this point.

The Lord could have told us more about Abram as an individual, but the story highlights something very important: God's salvation blessings never come because of our achievements,

"In this book Jonathan Griffiths leads us through the life of Abraham. As Christians we are pilgrims in a hostile world. So was Abraham. We can learn so much from his example. But there is a bigger story. Jonathan helps us see how God's dealings with Abraham prepared for the coming of Jesus, through whom all people have been blessed. He writes in a pastoral manner as he seeks to help us understand God's Word. It will deepen your knowledge and warm your heart."

PAUL MALLARD, FIEC Director for the West Midlands, and author of *Learning to Lament* and *An Anchor for the Soul*

"Jonathan Griffiths' guide to the life of Abraham is a delightful mix of close attention to the Bible text and real life application to warm the heart and stir us to action. It's constantly centered on and driven by the bigger gospel story. The clarity of writing also makes it very useful for preachers preparing a series on these rich chapters in Genesis. I highly commend this study."

JEREMY MCQUOID, Teaching Pastor, Deeside Christian Fellowship, and Chair of Trustees, Keswick Ministries

"This is biographical Bible exposition at its best. It is firmly rooted in Scripture and geared to our contemporary world and experience. As you read, you will be nourished and spoken to, as I was."

AJITH FERNANDO, Teaching Director, Youth for Christ, Sri Lanka, and author of *Discipling in a Multicultural World*

"As Jonathan leads us sure-footedly through the life of Abraham, he points us consistently to our wonderful God and his promises, and also to our Lord Jesus Christ, prefigured here. This book will be a help to any readers of Genesis, including preachers; it helps us approach the text responsibly and includes much helpful pastoral application. I found myself looking forward to picking it up every time."

ALASDAIR PAINE, Vicar, St Andrew the Great, Cambridge

STRANGERS & EXILES

JONATHAN GRIFFITHS

STRANGERS & EXILES

Pursuing faithfulness as pilgrims in a faithless world

EP

First published in Great Britain in 2024

British Library Cataloguing in Publication Data
A record for this book is available from the British Library

ISBN: 978-1-78397-434-4
Designed by Jude May
Cover image © Natalya Nepran | iStock

Printed in Denmark

Evangelical Press, an imprint of 10Publishing
Unit C, Tomlinson Road, Leyland, PR25 2DY, England
Email: epbooks@10ofthose.com
Website: www.10ofthose.com/ www.epbooks.org

1 3 5 7 10 8 6 4 2

For Hugo

Contents

Introduction: Strangers and Exiles

The journey of the earthly pilgrim walking with the Lord on the dusty trails of this world is rarely smooth or straight or easy. We do not need to walk with the Lord for long to know that this is true. Each one of us who walks this journey must learn over time the dynamics and realities of it, not least dynamics of our own frailties and of the Lord's great faithfulness. We learn these through the declarations of the Bible—through its statements of propositional truth—but we learn them as well through the stories of the Bible. We learn them through tracing the storyline of the Lord's calling and keeping and using of frail, feeble and flawed human beings—human beings like us.

Abraham is a foundational figure in the history of Israel and the church, a justly famous follower of the Lord and servant of the God of heaven. But he is at the same time profoundly human and raw and real. In his story, we see what it means for the Lord to take hold of a sinner, call him, privilege him with his promises, uphold him in his power, bear with him in his mercy, use him in his service, and sustain him to the end. Abraham trusts the Lord and Abraham fails the Lord. Abraham shows integrity and strength, compromise and weakness. And the Lord achieves his purposes in him and through him.

More than all this, in these key chapters of the book of Genesis, God sets out the pattern of salvation in the call of Abraham and, in varied ways, points through him to the greater Leader and Servant of his people who was to come. In Abraham we see a multi-dimensional but unpolished pattern of our own discipleship—and we see a hope-filled but imperfect foreshadowing of the Lord Jesus Christ.

It is my hope that this study will first and foremost nourish your soul as it deepens your knowledge of the Lord and his Word. I would encourage you to read it Bible in hand, reading first the chapters of Genesis that the chapters of this book treat. I believe that it could make a good basis for personal devotion or a group study. Secondarily, but significantly, I hope that Bible teachers who plan to tackle the Abraham narrative will find in these pages some pointers and insight for the exposition of this portion of the Word of God—and in that way, I trust that there might be a wider benefit to those who sit under their teaching.

1

Blessed to be a blessing

Genesis 12

When things go wrong or relationships turn sour, it is wonderful if an opportunity comes along to make a fresh start. I suspect all of us, at one time or another, have longed for that chance. A partnership, a friendship, a business venture, a new project—it started so well, but then things went off balance. If only we could put things right.

The book of Genesis begins in beauty, innocence, and hope, with a good and gracious God, and a world full of promise. But things soon take a darker turn and the beautiful tapestry of life as God created it to be begins to fray. The people God created as the crowning glory of his work start to doubt his goodness and refuse to live his way in his world. God responds to their sin by placing them and the world under judgment. He sends the man and woman out of the Garden of Eden, and they face the prospect of life in a chaotic world, outside the immediate presence of God. We see things quickly go from bad to worse. As sin takes hold, relationships break down, and the order of God's good world is disrupted. Chaos and acrimony set in, and death soon swallows up life itself.

God eventually decides he will have no more of it, and he wipes out life on the earth with a great flood, sparing only Noah, his family, and the animals on the ark. There is a fresh start for Noah and his family, but all too soon we find Noah falling into drunkenness and shame, and the downward spiral resumes. The low point comes in Genesis 11 with the Tower of Babel, where people in their arrogance seek to make a name for themselves, even trying to ascend to God's own place in heaven. God judges their pride and arrogance by mixing up their languages and scattering the nations in confusion.

It is against this backdrop that we read of the fresh start of Genesis 12. It is a glorious and thrilling fresh start. It is the fresh start that establishes the foundation of the gospel, giving hope not just to one nation, but to all the nations. God declares that sin and judgment and death will not be the end of the human story, but will give way to a wonderful plan of redemption. The story of Genesis 12 is the story of a very great blessing.

Thus far in Genesis we have seen the good world God made come under judgment for sin But here in Genesis 12, we have an emphatic and gracious new start. Five times, God speaks blessing on Abram and his family. "I will bless you… and you will be a blessing… I will bless those who bless you… in you all the families of the earth shall be blessed" (verses 1–3). The story of Abram is one of a great blessing that comes in the place of curse. It is a fresh start that takes place amid pain, loss and the sheer wreckage of sin. It is a story of hope and, ultimately, a story of salvation.

But we are getting ahead of ourselves. Abram's story begins in simplicity, and perhaps a degree of obscurity. A man named Terah lived in a place called Ur of the Chaldeans, located in modern day Iraq. He had three sons, one of them named Abram (11:27). He planned to move with his family to the land of Canaan, but instead, they stopped in a place called Haran, goodness or moral record. What we see in Abram is a pattern that is repeated throughout the Bible: God gives salvation and bestows his kindness because he has chosen to do so—because he is gracious, because he is kind. Abram was born into a world broken and ruined by sin, and at a low point in human history. But God intervened, and because of his gracious work, the situation was radically changed. A life was redirected, a nation was established, a Savior came, the good news went out, and the church was born. God acted on his own initiative and out of his own grace. We too are part of the ruined race, participants in the downward spiral of sin, citizens of this stricken world. Yet God comes to us in Christ and speaks to us in the gospel, offering us salvation blessings. He invites us to be part of his family, and beckons us to his eternal home above. Not because we have done anything to catch his attention or earn his favor, but simply because he is kind.

For those of us who have been walking with the Lord for some time, this is a truth for us too if we are in any way tempted to think that we have placed ourselves in a position of special favor with God by serving well, following faithfully, and giving generously. Those things are good, but they are not the basis of anything in the sight of God. The only starting point is the kindness of God. Everything else is response.

God's blessings come with a call to respond

We are often called upon to believe unbelievable things. Just the other day I received an email with the happy news that the International Monetary Fund wished to compensate me $1.5 million because of fraud I had apparently suffered. I only needed to provide $3,000 to cover administrative costs and the monies would be deposited into my account without delay. The message was pure nonsense, of course. It is worth registering the apparent impossibility of all that God is calling Abram to take on board here. He is calling him to leave everything—his family, security, and land—and go to an unknown place. God is promising that he will be father to a great nation. It all seems so unlikely, so against the odds. Abram is 75, rather old for having kids. More than that, his wife Sarai is barren (11:30). It is almost laughable that this couple should believe they will produce offspring, let alone a whole nation. The land that is promised is already occupied by the Canaanites (verse 6), and before too long, a famine will strike the land, and they will need to look elsewhere for food (verse 10). It is challenge after challenge, obstacle after obstacle. But God, without hesitation, irony, or embarrassment calls Abram to believe and go. And Abram went, "as the LORD had told him" (verse 4). In the gospel, God promises to take the messy lives of sinful people like us, and, because of the death and resurrection of his Son, forgive us, accept us, and welcome us into his family. He promises to bring us to his heavenly home and pour his kindness upon us in all eternity.

As we look at the mess of our lives, we wonder if the miracle of forgiveness can be true. We hear promises of heaven and eternal life and wonder if it is just a fairy tale. We hear the promise that God will take us all the way home, and we look out at the hard road ahead with its challenges, difficulties and griefs on the way. We wonder if the journey is actually feasible. We wonder if we can persevere. And then there is the question of our own comfort here and now. Later in verse 5, we discover that Abram had actually done quite well for himself in Haran. When Abram and his household left their home at the Lord's command, it sounds like they needed a little fleet of moving trucks. The shipping containers were lined up on the driveway. Abram and Sarai had quite the set-up in their own country, quite the household. Yet the call was to pack up everything, leave their support networks and their prosperous livelihood and go to an unknown place.

The writer of Hebrews sees in this a remarkable model of faith:

> "By faith Abraham obeyed when he was called to go out to a place that he was to receive as an inheritance. And he went out, not knowing where he was going. By faith he went to live in the land of promise, as in a foreign land, living in tents… For he was looking forward to the city that has foundations, whose designer and builder is God" (Hebrews 11:8–10).

Abram was a man of faith. He was not expecting a nice piece of real estate in the ancient land of Canaan. No, his eyes were set on eternity; he was looking to a more permanent home in the city above. Because of that, he was willing to do something that, humanly speaking, looked ill-advised. He was willing to leave his home, his extended family, his support networks, and all that was familiar to go to a place he did not know.

In all this, Abram is indeed a model of faith for us. As we put our hand in the hand of the Lord Jesus by faith and entrust our life to him, we are turning our back on the familiar, the tangible, the apparently safe, and we are entrusting ourselves to the promises of God. We are relying on his blessing and setting our sights on an unseen homeland above. We see that kind of faith years later in the response of the fishermen to Jesus. He issues to them the call to "Follow me, and I will make you fishers of men" (Matthew 4:19), and immediately they leave their nets, their livelihood and their homes and follow him. We see that kind of faith in stories today of those who have heard the call to follow Jesus and have quite literally had to leave their families because they have been rejected by them for their faith. We see it in those who have left their homes to make Jesus known in unfamiliar, far-flung, and hostile places. We see it in those who have left financial security and worldly ambition to serve in the work of the gospel. We see it in any who have decided to trust in Jesus, hope for heaven, and set aside the drive for success or fulfilment or wealth in this world.

In the gospel, the call is the same for us as it was for Abram. Have you heard that call to follow Jesus, to trust him, and to set your sights on heaven above? If you have already responded to that invitation in years past, are you still trusting the promises of God, delighting in his blessings, holding lightly to this present world, and longing for the home he has prepared for us?

God's blessings come to a flawed and sinful people

It is amazing how quickly things go wrong when Abram decides to follow God's leading. He gets to Canaan, the place of God's calling and God's will, and sets about making altars to the Lord here, there and everywhere, claiming the land for the Lord. We might now expect showers of blessing. We tend to anticipate that things will go smoothly when we are on a mission for the Lord, but it is rarely like that. Trouble strikes quickly: "Now there was a famine in the land" (verse 10). That was not what we expected. That certainly was not in the travel brochure. This was no minor heatwave or a few dry days, this was a severe famine. There were no clouds in the sky for day after day, week after week. The green fields had become dustbowls. If you had looked at the herds, you would have seen gaunt figures with ribcages on display, cattle dying for lack of water. Children are going hungry and crying for food.

How can this be the Lord's plan and the place of the Lord's blessing? Abram might start to remember how good things had been in Haran. He had built up wealth there, he was prosperous. In Canaan, he found he had to deal with the Canaanites, he had to trek around setting up altars and claiming the land for the Lord, battling no doubt against godless opposition. The land of blessing turns out to be not so blessed, it seems.

Maybe you have had an experience that resonates with this. The Lord calls you to follow him, and it is exciting and joyful. But, no sooner do you trust in Jesus and commit your life to him, than things start to get a whole lot harder and more complicated. The life of blessing starts to look like a life of trial and heartache. Or you sense the Lord leading you to a new area of Christian service, a new ministry or a new mission field. You embrace the cost and risk and sign on, perhaps quitting your day job, taking a financial hit, moving your family. You anticipate the blessing of the Lord but, immediately, difficulty descends or disaster strikes. You find yourself asking, *What is going on, Lord?*

The time of pressure becomes a time of testing, a time of vulnerability. In Abram's case, we see that it also quickly becomes a time of failure and a time of sin:

> "When he was about to enter Egypt, he said to Sarai his wife, 'I know that you are a woman beautiful in appearance, and when the Egyptians see you, they will say, "This is his wife." Then they will kill me, but they will let you live. Say you are my sister, that it may go well with me because of you, and that my life may be spared for your sake'" (verses 11–13).

Here is the great hero of faith, the man at the very center of God's plans not just for the nation of Israel, but for the world. He is God's man to overturn the damage of sin and to make a glorious new start. He is at the very beginning of a great venture with the Lord and for the Lord. What does he do next? He makes a catastrophic and sinful mess of it.

Abram is under pressure. He has got to get food for the family. He has got to manage a crisis. Now he is presented with a challenging and difficult situation, and he decides to leave the land of promise and head to Egypt. We wonder if that is wise. Abram is going into a hostile and godless land. As he goes in, he fears that the people will have no scruples. He is aware that his wife is beautiful and that some Egyptian man might decide he wants the husband out of the way. Rather than protect the honor of his wife and the sanctity of his own marriage, Abram does something that seems both cowardly and deceitful. He says, *Let's pretend we are not married, so that if some Egyptian wants to marry you, they will not beat me up to get to you. How about that, Sarai?*

We learn later in Genesis that Sarai was Abram's half-sister (20:12), so it is a half-truth he tells here. But the whole maneuver looks cowardly and self-serving. Abram is concerned for *numero uno* above all else. Just notice what he says: *If we do not do this, Sarai, they will kill me, but let you live. Just say you are my sister,* "that it may go well with me because of you" (verse 13). *You may be forcibly taken by some Egyptian, but I think I will be ok.* The plan works out perfectly:

> "When Abram entered Egypt, the Egyptians saw that the woman was very beautiful. And when the princes of Pharaoh saw her, they praised her to Pharaoh. And the woman was taken into Pharaoh's house. And for her sake he dealt well with Abram; and he had sheep, oxen, male donkeys, male servants, female servants, female donkeys, and camels" (verses 14–16).

Sarai's dignity is reduced to nothing; she is taken into Pharaoh's hareem. But Abram does well out of the deal. Since his sister is now a wife of the king, he is lavished with riches. Whatever pangs of regret he may feel, they are soothed by his immensely increased wealth. It seems to be going well, but that is only for the short term. Although Pharaoh does not know it, he has become guilty of participating in adultery and God judges him and his household with plagues. Pharoah soon discovers what has really gone on and summons Abram for an explanation. Pharaoh proceeds in a markedly decent manner, particularly in comparison with Abram. Rather than punish Abram, he sends the whole lot of them on their way, with all the riches they had gained in the process. And so, Abram ends up back where he should have been, back in the Promised Land—all because Pharaoh has expelled him from Egypt.

It is a dark chapter in the story of Abram's life. The hero of faith immediately becomes a catastrophic failure of discipleship. It is sordid, cowardly, and ugly. It is a shocking way to end one of the most hope-filled, promise-rich, theologically significant chapters of the Bible. Why did it go like this? What is the Lord teaching us here?

He is driving home the point that Abram is not the hero of the story. Salvation comes from the Lord himself and him alone. Salvation is God's plan, God's blessing, and God's gift. The hero of this story, and of every story in the Bible, is God himself. Salvation is never something that we earn. Abram did not earn God's blessings. Even if he had somehow earned them at the start of chapter 12, he would surely have lost them by the end of the chapter due to his failure and sin. God's blessings are never earned, they are only given by his grace.

We need this reminder. We are all messy and sinful characters who get things wrong. If the first recipient of God's blessing had been a flawless hero and Abram's record had been perfect, we might assume that we would never be good enough to receive the saving blessings of God. But the gospel reality is that God chooses to save and bless weak, flawed, and sinful people. The failures of God's people do not stop his saving plan. Abram might have feared that his compromise and cowardice in Egypt would derail God's plan to bring blessing to the world through him, but wonderfully, that was not so. We may feel that we have made a mess of things in our Christian discipleship. We may look back on sin and foolishness and wonder if we have rendered ourselves useless in God's service and a hindrance to his mission. But Abram teaches us that God does not give up on failures easily. He does not cast aside his blessed and saved people. He still uses us for significant work within his kingdom. If you are staring some kind of compromise or failure in the face and wondering if your life can still be of use to God, consider Abram in Egypt. Abram's story goes on. Let that reassure you of the patience and kindness of God and take heart today.

God's salvation blessings *come by his initiative and grace*—praise God. They *come with a call to respond in faith*. Have you responded to that call? Are you still heeding that call today? They *come to a flawed and sinful people*, and that means there is hope for you and for me. There is a place for each one of us—*even us*—in the plans and purposes of God.

2

The open hand of faith

Genesis 13

As God's people walk in faith through the territories of this world toward their promised homeland, there will be different ways in which faith is tried and tested. That was true for Abram, and of course, it is true for us. In Genesis 12, the very first test that Abram faces after receiving God's covenant promises is the test of material want, in the form of a famine (12:10). Back in the early part of chapter 12, Abram is in a good place, geographically and spiritually. The Lord reaffirms the promise that he will give him this land. As a sign of his commitment to the Lord, Abram builds an altar (12:7). From there he goes to the hill country between Bethel and Ai and builds another altar and calls upon the name of the Lord (12:8). He then travels to the Negeb (12:9). From there, he makes the ill-fated journey down to Egypt. But notice the return pilgrimage that he undertakes, both geographical and spiritual. First, he goes up from Egypt to the Negeb (13:1). Then he journeys on "as far as Bethel to the place where his tents had been at the beginning, between Bethel and Ai, to the place where he had made the altar at the first. And there Abram called upon the name of the LORD" (verses 3–4). It is a complete re-tracing of his steps, back to the land of promise, back to the altar he made—and back to a place of much greater spiritual health. The geographical re-set mirrors the spiritual re-set of his heart.

We see so clearly the abundant grace of God in this. Abram stumbles badly in chapter 12. It is all a mess. But the Lord does not let him fall completely. He is not done with him. He graciously picks Abram up and sets him back on the path of faith and obedience. Look at the opportunity Abram is given to re-trace his steps and get back into the spiritual saddle. Take a moment to rejoice in it, because in this, there is hope for us too. If God did not give up on Abram after his big stumble in Egypt, then surely this same God will not too easily give up on us when we make a mess of things, as we so often do—when we are sinful and foolish, as we often are. Chapter 13 begins with an encouragement for the stumbling, the sinful, and the foolish. Perhaps for some, that is just the encouragement we need.

The crisis of Genesis 12 was a crisis of material need, but the crisis of Genesis 13 arises from material prosperity. The narrative begins: "Now Abram was very rich in livestock, in silver, and in gold" (verse 2). Abram was prosperous before ever he went to Canaan, but Abram had progressed from being *rich* (12:16) to being *very rich*. As we will see, it is the challenge of abundance that will define Genesis 13.[1] What will Abram do when faced with material abundance, when faced with a choice about how to respond to the opportunities of wealth? It is a fascinating predicament, perhaps one you might feel you would be willing to sign up for yourself! Hardly a bad problem to have, we might think. Nonetheless we will find that this test takes us to the heart of what it means to know the Lord, to wait upon his promises, and to hope for his eternal inheritance.

A situation arises because of sheer abundance. Abram has brought his nephew Lot with him on this pilgrimage, and they have built up quite an entourage. Abram is now very rich and so, evidently, is Lot:

> "Lot… also had flocks and herds and tents, so that the land could not support both of them dwelling together; for their possessions were so great that they could not dwell together, and there was strife between the herdsmen of Abram's livestock and the herdsmen of Lot's livestock" (verses 5–7).

This family has become so prosperous that they cannot all live in one place. To make room for their abundance, they need to split from one another and settle in different regions. On one level, it seems a nice problem to have. What follows is a discussion about who will go where. It is easy to imagine that this is simply about a real estate deal, or an inheritance negotiation, or a bit of family politics. But we need to remember that we are dealing with no ordinary family and no ordinary inheritance. Abram and his family are heirs of the salvation promises of God, and the land of Canaan is at the heart of those promises and a great symbol of that inheritance. The attitude of both Abram and Lot toward this land reveals something deeper about them and their response to the Lord. It teaches us something fundamental about what it means to be a people who set our hope on God's covenant promises.[2]

Genesis 13 sets out a stark contrast between the two men. Let's look at each of them in turn.

Lot: the closed fist of materialism

Abram sees the problem before him and proposes a solution in verses 8–9, saying, in essence: *Let's not have a fight here over the family inheritance. We can't all have grandma's diamond ring. We can't all move into the old family home. We can't all live in this part of the land. Let's go our separate ways and divide things up. Why don't you choose, Lot?* It is interesting that Abram does this, because he could argue that the land had been promised to him and his descendants, and that his nephew does not really count. But Abram is treating him as part of his own family and is being more than generous. Lot does not hesitate to take Abram up on the offer. There is no tussle of any kind here.

I remember going for a meal at a local restaurant called The Swiss Chalet with some of our extended family when I was a child. This was in the days when the bill came on a little plastic tray with a pen, so that you could sign to guarantee the payment. When the bill was brought to our table, my father and uncle both tried to get hold of the little tray before the other. They knew they would have to act fast if they wanted to pay, and the plastic tray cracked in half as they both grabbed it. I do not know who paid, and I do not know if they got billed extra for the broken tray, but the incident sticks in my mind.

There was no similar tussle here in Canaan. Abram began with a gracious offer and Lot was all too ready to take him up on it:

> "Lot lifted up his eyes and saw that the Jordan Valley was well watered everywhere like the garden of the Lord, like the land of Egypt, in the direction of Zoar… So, Lot chose for himself all the Jordan Valley, and Lot journeyed east. Thus, they separated from one another" (verses 10–11).

Lot lifts his eyes and there is a twinkle of joy and anticipation. It is the look of someone leafing through a luxury real estate magazine over coffee and just imagining what might be. But as we follow Lot's gaze, we detect some signs of trouble. We soon hear notes of warning. Lot sees the valley of the Jordan River.

It is well watered and green. The herds would flourish there. In fact, it is so lush and beautiful that it is reminiscent of a place now closed to the human race—the now forbidden Garden of Eden. Lot thinks to himself, *This is like the Garden; this is heaven on earth.* Moreover, this is a lot like Egypt, the place that had been a refuge to the family not so long ago. But Lot did not consider the fact that the fertile, lush, well-watered land of Egypt was never a friendly place for the people of God. It would be a place of danger for generations to come.

The valley of the Jordan River would put Lot at the very edge of the Promised Land, if not outside it. We feel more and more uneasy as we follow Lot's wandering eye, but the terrifying note comes in the brackets at the end of verse 10: "This was before the Lord destroyed Sodom and Gomorrah." The outcome for those cities is well known; they will be destroyed in a great act of judgment. It is a foreboding mention and speaks of trouble to come. The text makes clear just how godless a place it is: "Now the men of Sodom were wicked, great sinners against the Lord" (verse 13). Nonetheless, it is where Lot chooses to go: "So Lot chose for himself all the Jordan Valley, and Lot journeyed east" (verse 11). As we are seeing, geographical movements end up being spiritually significant. They tell us something about the heart. This is true for both Abram and Lot. Lot headed "east," and that is meaningful in Genesis.

When Adam and Eve sinned against the Lord and were expelled from the Garden, they headed east: "He drove out the man, and at the east of the garden of Eden he placed a cherub and a flaming sword" (3:24). When Cain killed his brother Abel, we read that "Cain went away from the presence of the Lord and settled in the land of Nod, east of Eden" (4:16). It was a people who had been journeying in the east who decided to build the Tower of Babel (11:2).

To head east in the geography of Genesis often means trouble. It is not that west is better than east in some objective sense, of course, but here in the narrative of Genesis it seems that east is where you go if you are heading away from the Lord. What was going on with Lot? It is clear that his main interest was *not* to be safely within the territory of Canaan, in the land of promise. He ventured to the very edge of the land. He possibly went outside it. His choice of territory was based on just one thing: he wanted to find paradise on earth. He wanted the most beautiful and most fertile, productive land he could find. On one level, that sounds fine. Why not, after all? We are meant to see that Lot was working purely on a physical and material plane. And because of that, the Lord and his promises were not on his mind, nor was his uncle Abram and his needs. Lot was going to take whatever he could get, because the physical land and the wealth that would flow from it were his top priority.

What Lot did not anticipate was where all this would take him. We are told in 13:12 that he moved his tent as far as Sodom. By the next chapter, we learn that Lot is "dwelling" in Sodom, in the wicked city itself (14:12). By chapter 19, when the angels come to warn Lot of the city's destruction, he has well and truly made his home there.[3] Calvin writes that "Lot, when he fancied he was living in paradise, was nearly plunged into the depths of hell."[4] He thought he had chosen for himself a little piece of heaven but, in fact, he had started a journey on the road leading to destruction. That is Lot, with the closed fist of the materialist. He grabbed what he wanted from this world, without regard for the Lord and his promises, or his relative, and he held on tight. In so doing, he set himself on a dangerous spiritual path.

Abram: the open hand of faith

In 2020, London's *Financial Times* reported that the "Number of contested wills [is] at an all-time high as rising house prices and complex structures drive competing claims."[5] Maybe you have seen or experienced an inheritance dispute among family. It can be very messy. When a family comes to divide up a shared inheritance, it is rare to find someone who takes Abram's approach as he spoke to Lot: "Let there be no strife between you and me, and between your herdsmen and my herdsmen, for we are kinsmen" (verse 8). *We are family here,* says Abram, *we don't need to fight over land.* "Is not the whole land before you? Separate yourself from me. If you take the left hand, then I will go to the right, or if you take the right hand, then I will go to the left" (verse 9). *You choose, Lot. You take what you want, and I will just fit in and take what remains.* It is one thing if an inheritance consists of an ugly painting, a 20-year-old Chevy, and a battered old sofa. *Take what you want. No problem.* But the asset here is prime real estate. Still, Abram is open-handed, generous and gracious. *Lot, take what you want.* What was Abram doing? How could he do this?

Was he saying that the land did not matter to him? Was he saying that he did not care for what God was giving him? As we look at Abram and his life, we must draw a different conclusion. Although this land mattered to Abram, something else mattered even more. His eyes were fixed elsewhere. Hebrews 11 explains how Abram was able to behave in this way:

> "By faith Abraham obeyed when he was called to go out to a place that he was to receive as an inheritance. And he went out, not knowing where he was going. By faith he went to live in the land of promise, as in a foreign land, living in tents with Isaac and Jacob, heirs with him of the same promise. *For he was looking forward to the city that has foundations, whose designer and builder is God"* (Hebrews 11:8–10, my emphasis).

Abram was able to hold loosely to his inheritance in this world because he knew that there was something even greater to come. He was looking forward to the eternal city and his eternal home. Because his hope was in the Lord, he was able to open his hand in generosity with the things of this world. And notice the outcome for him:

> "The LORD said to Abram, after Lot had separated from him, 'Lift up your eyes and look from the place where you are, northward and southward and eastward and westward, for all the land that you see I will give to you and your offspring forever'" (verses 14–15).

Remember how Lot lifted up his eyes in verse 10 and set his heart upon his patch of territory in the east? Now the Lord himself lifts up Abram's eyes and says, *Look east and west and north and south. All of it will be yours. I am reaffirming my promise to you. And let me make it clearer: you will not just have offspring; you will have so many that they will be like the dust of the earth. They will be uncountable. Go and wander the full length of the land. All of it will be yours.* The account ends with Abram pitching his tents and building an altar to the Lord. On one level, it is a simple incident—two members of a family dividing some real estate that has been given as an inheritance. One of them, focused on this present world, seeks to grab his little slice of heaven here below, but it turns out that his pilgrimage takes him down a road bound for destruction. Another, with eyes set on eternity and heart set on the Lord and his promises, opens his hand in generosity. The Lord, in response, prospers him.

What does all this hold for us? Is it to be a model of how to handle wealth, family disputes or a shared inheritance? We would, no doubt, do well to learn from Abram in these things. But again, we need to look at the big picture. Remember who

Abram is. He is the man whom God has chosen to bless and, through him, to bring salvation blessings to a lost and dying world (12:3). This will happen, ultimately, through great Abram's greater Son. This whole story leads us to a stable in Bethlehem, to a cross at Calvary, and to a throne on high. In Abram, we see something of the Lord Jesus himself. We see one who is heir to all things, yet who holds them lightly because he knows and trusts the Father. We see one who will bless others at great cost to himself. We see one who will bear that cost because he is looking to the future. We see the pattern of the one who is to come, a hint of how this family blessing will come to the world.

The narrative reminds us of the Son who was taken by the devil to a high place and shown all the glittering kingdoms of the world. It reminds us how he was tempted to grasp that which was already his own and to pledge allegiance to the devil in doing so, but who refused to press that claim (Matthew 4:1–11).[6] It reminds us of the one Paul tells us about:

> "…who, though he was in the form of God, did not count equality with God a thing to be grasped, but emptied himself, by taking the form of a servant, being born in the likeness of men. And being found in human form, he humbled himself by becoming obedient to the point of death, even death on a cross" (Philippians 2:6–8).

The salvation blessings of God come to the world, not through one who grasps at what is his, but through one who sets aside what he might rightfully claim. They come through the one who willingly bears the cost and becomes a servant to those who would go the way of destruction. The salvation blessings of God come through an heir, a precious Son, who does not stand on his rights, but who freely gives. Abram models that in a small way, and Jesus perfects it at the cross. We are, of course, recipients of that kindness. Although we would love to put ourselves in Abram's shoes, our natural inclination is to be much more like Lot. But in Jesus, we have freely received an inheritance that is not rightly ours. This is the essence of the offer of the gospel for us: forgiveness through the blood of Christ, a future, an inheritance—all through the generosity of Christ.

We need to see that this radical generosity that saves us must also *shape us*. If we have received this and, like Abram, are heirs of the great promises of God, we must be those who learn to hold loosely to the rights and privileges and possessions of this world. We must be those whose hands are open, whose fists are not clenched. We need to be like that if we are to be messengers who bring the salvation blessings of God to a perishing world.

Not long ago, my wife and I participated in an online memorial service for a friend who died in a tragic accident. This man was in his mid-40s, with a wife and children, serving as a missionary church-planter in a spiritually hard, European capital city. He was from the United States, from a prominent and prosperous American family. He was outstandingly gifted and capable, and it was noted at his memorial that he could have done just about anything he wanted with his life: politics, business, you name it. But the grace of God got hold of him. The gospel took root in his life and God gave him a burden for the nation where he ultimately served. He elected to become a missionary and to settle in a foreign land with his young family. If you want to find a job with zero prestige and meagre pay, let me encourage you to become a Protestant missionary in a historically Catholic but currently aggressively atheistic country. This is not the route to riches or fame. But wonderfully, this man left a legacy in European missions, and the work he began in church planting and training pastors will go on.

Genesis 13 shows us that this is the gospel pattern. It is the way it has always been. The promises of God come through his

Word, the grace of God gets hold of a heart, there is an open hand with respect to the things of this world, and God's salvation blessings flow out to the nations. How is your hold on the things of this world today? What does your claim on your rights and possessions say about your trust in the Word of God? What does it say about your hope in the promises of God, about your delight in the future that God has set before his people? How might he use you in his great gospel plan for the nations as you hold those things with an open hand, as Abram did?

3

Battle and blessing

Genesis 14

One of the perplexing things about God's work in bringing his plans and purposes to fruition is that progress rarely seems smooth. How many pages of the Bible can you find where there is no trouble whatsoever, no threat, no opposition? How many chapters are there of plain sailing? Genesis 14 comes just three chapters into the history of Israel and the story of Abram, and already there has been an environmental crisis (the famine), a moral and spiritual crisis (as Abram and Sarai chose to deceive Pharoah), a political crisis (arising from the deception), and a potential family crisis (Lot and Abram dividing the inheritance). Now there is a military crisis as well, in the form of a regional, multi-national war of fearful potential. With the foundational salvation promises of God having been given in chapter 12, these early chapters of the story of Israel in the life of Abram show us how the salvation plan of God will move forward in the world.

God's saving purposes move forward in the messiness of history

Have you ever gone away to a Christian retreat center for a few days and enjoyed that feeling of stepping away from the real world? You have time with other believers, teaching from God's Word, and the chance to switch off a little to the brokenness and chaos we see all around us. It can be a little taste of heaven. We sometimes imagine that people in the Bible lived like that all the time. They were living at the center of the action of the salvation story, after all, whereas we must grapple daily with the real and very complicated world of the 21st century, in all its profound messiness. But when we come to Genesis 14, we soon see that things were messy in those days too.

As we start to read the story, we may wonder why God has given us so much historical detail here. Why so many unfamiliar names of foreign kings and places that we are unable to pinpoint on a map? Why so many pronunciation challenges for us modern readers? As we pay attention to the text, we discern a basic narrative. The little Canaanite kingdoms have been under the thumb of Chedorlaomer who has led a coalition of foreign powers from Mesopotamia for a dozen years. The Canaanite kings eventually get tired of the situation and rebel. However, it does not go well for them. The Mesopotamian kings, led by Chedorlaomer, come back and crush them. The Canaanite kings then flee, leaving the cities of Sodom and Gomorrah to be plundered.

I have a nephew who loves military history and devours great tomes about the First and the Second World Wars, and all the details of the various battles. That is the kind of information we are being given here. But it is not the precise details of individual battles that matter. In this first half of chapter 14, it is as though we are being shown a report from the *Times of Canaan* or from the *Sodom Gazette*, summarizing the details of the great confrontation that has consumed the region. The description of all this messy historical detail is revealing something fundamental: the plan of salvation does not unfold in the comfortable Christian retreat center, tucked away from the unpleasant realities of life in this fallen world. No, it unfolds in the middle of the mess and chaos of human history. Abram and his family are buffeted by the storms of life and the destabilizing currents of geopolitics. The fighting has evidently been going on at some distance from Abram and his immediate clan. But his nephew Lot has been perilously close to the action. In chapter 13, we saw how Lot had taken the fateful decision to settle in the vicinity of Sodom. It turns out that it was not a great place to be:

> "So the enemy took all the possessions of Sodom and Gomorrah, and all their provisions, and went their way. They also took Lot, the son of Abram's brother, who was dwelling in Sodom, and his possessions, and went their way" (verses 11–12).

With the covenant promises of Genesis 12 still ringing in our ears, we might have assumed that the family of Abram would be enjoying God's blessings in an uninterrupted way, settling down in peace in the land of promise. But in this unfolding crisis, Lot (who is the closest thing that Abram has to an heir) has been captured by enemy forces and his very survival is in serious doubt. And we think to ourselves, *This is not how things are meant to unfold for the family of God. It is not how the life of faith is meant to go.* But Genesis 14 takes us in a direction we might not have anticipated. God's salvation plan unfolds as history itself unfolds. However chaotic things look in the cut and thrust of geopolitical and world events, however messy things look on the smudged and tattered page of human history, God's plans are not disrupted or derailed.

We need to take that insight from ancient Canaan in Abram's day and transpose it to our own day. The mess of life in this world, the apparent chaos of pandemics, financial meltdowns, political upheavals, wars and rumors of wars, and all the rest—none of it has the capacity to undermine the plans and purposes of God. For God's people to have to learn to trust him during such things is not strange or surprising. This is how it has always been, ever since the departure from Eden. This is precisely where God does his work and unfolds his greater plan. As 21st-century people, we have lived through a disruptive and damaging pandemic. We are experiencing political turmoil, and great social and economic upheaval. War is never absent from the global scene. The messiness of this world, the chaos of our age, and the carnage of sin in all its variety impacts our lives and ministries, the discipleship of our families and our gospel witness to our friends. It impacts our own growth as Christians. But here is the encouragement: it is in precisely such situations that God's people live and grow and serve. It is in messy situations that God's salvation plan moves forward. This is not strange or new. It is the way it has always been. The smudged and tattered page of human history is the page upon which God writes the story of his saving work.

God's saving purposes move forward by a gracious rescue

The government of Barbados proceeded with a long-discussed plan to remove the British monarch as the head of state in 2021. It had been in the works for a long time and came as no surprise to anyone. Many other former colonies have taken the same path. But imagine if, soon after separation, Barbados came under military siege by a hostile foreign power. Imagine if the president of Barbados then picked up the phone to London and said, "It turns out we are in some trouble here. Could you send over some help? We have got enemy ships surrounding us. Could you send the Royal Navy to assist?" I do not know how these things work but you could imagine the British government thinking: *Hold on. We just had a rather awkward separation. This part of the family moved on. Now we are being asked to put our forces in danger to rescue them. Do we want to do that?*

Abram and Lot had a rather awkward separation back in Genesis 13. We saw how Lot headed for the territory that looked pleasant and prosperous without taking much account of the Lord's provision. He moved to the eastern edge of the Promised Land, and even beyond. Sodom, the city near the place where he settled, became known chiefly for its sin. Abram could well have considered Lot to be selfish, silly, and unwise. He could have been insulted and disappointed, offended and hurt. Maybe he was. We do not know. But now Abram hears that Lot is in big trouble. Helping him would be costly, inconvenient, and positively perilous.

This becomes a moment of distinction and triumph for Abram:

> "When Abram heard that his kinsman had been taken captive, he led forth his trained men, born in his house, 318 of them and went in pursuit as far as Dan. And he divided his forces against them by night, he and his servants, and defeated them and pursued them to Hobah, north of Damascus. Then he brought back all the possessions, and also brought back his kinsman Lot with his possessions, and the women and the people" (verses 14–16).

Abram hears the call. Rather than nurse his wounds about Lot's previous behavior and enjoy an "I-told-you-so" moment, he is gracious, kind, and full of sheer goodness. He leads his trained men and goes in pursuit. Yes, he and Lot had separated. Yes, Lot seemed to have little regard for the promises of God. Yes, Lot had chosen the best territory for himself, without a thought for his uncle. But Abram knows that Lot is still his kinsman, and he is not about to let him perish at the hands of his enemies.

We could look at Abram here and draw a direct moral lesson from him for ourselves: Abram was gracious to the undeserving and we should be the same. It is a good moral lesson to take home. But before we go to a *moral lesson*, we need to notice the *gospel pattern*.[1] Remember that Abram is the recipient of the covenant blessings of God. The Lord has promised that he will bring blessing to the world through Abram. The *salvation blessings of God* are going to flow through this man and his family. And here, we see God using Abram to bring deliverance to an unwise and wayward nephew who got himself into a dangerous place through worldly thinking and behavior. As God's chosen servant, Abram looks at the situation and responds in a way that is right after God's own heart. He does not look for an easy excuse to ignore the situation, as others might. *Business is crazy just now... The staff are taking up so much time... I have got to focus on things at home... The situation looks too dangerous... too costly...* None of that. He enters the fray and resolves to bring deliverance.

When the Lord looked on his wayward children—on you and me, in our foolishness and sin, perishing because of the disastrous choices we have made—what did he do? Paul tells us:

> "For we ourselves were once foolish, disobedient, led astray, slaves to various passions and pleasures, passing our days in malice and envy, hated by others and hating one another. But when the goodness and loving kindness of God our Savior appeared, he saved us, not because of works done by us in righteousness, but according to his own mercy" (Titus 3:3–5).

> "For while we were still weak, at the right time Christ died for the ungodly. For one will scarcely die for a righteous person—though perhaps for a good person one would dare even to die—but God shows his love for us in that while we were still sinners, Christ died for us" (Romans 5:6–8).

God looked on us in our misery, our weakness and our sin, and he caused his lovingkindness to appear in the world, in the person of his Son, who came to be our rescuer. He did not stand far off from us when we were in distress. He came near, he showed his love, and he entered the mess of the battle. Ultimately, he died in our place that we might live.

In Abram here, we see something of the heart of God. We see a gracious gospel pattern. Once again, we would love to identify ourselves with Abram in his virtue and grace. But we should probably admit that Lot's shoes fit us a little better. By wandering from the safety of the Lord and his presence, like Lot, we put ourselves in grave danger. Like Lot, each one of us has gone down to the wicked city, as we have turned away from our Maker. But, praise God, the righteous Savior has come for us. Praise God, the righteous Savior has put his life on the line. And praise God, there is a deliverance for each one of us. This is the way God's salvation works. It is how his salvation blessings come to needy people like us.

I hope that you have a clear understanding of your need and I hope that you know this salvation. Apart from Christ, you would be in the grips of the forces of a powerful spiritual enemy who seeks not only to capture people but to destroy them. Are you rejoicing today in the gracious rescue that God has achieved for us in Christ? Are you rejoicing that he came down to Sodom, as it were, to save us from the forces of sin and evil that would destroy us? Does that truth thrill you and fill you with joy as much now as it ever did?

God's saving purposes move forward through a greater King

Every once in a while something great is eclipsed in its moment of glory by something greater. In the rush for green energy alternatives in 2011, the Crescent Dunes solar installation in

Nevada was touted as something of a marvel. The billion-dollar installation would be the biggest plant of its kind in the world and would produce enough electricity from the sun to power a whole city using ten thousand mirrors. It looked like the model solution for renewable power. But by the time the massive plant came online, new and more efficient solar panel technology had already eclipsed it. It was already obsolete and redundant. In its moment of glory, it was immediately outshone.[2]

Back in Genesis 3, the Lord made a promise to Eve that a descendent of hers would crush the head of the serpent. Ever since then, we scour the pages of Scripture looking for this Serpent-Crusher, this deliverer, this Savior.

Here in Genesis 14, we reach a moment of glory for Abram. With only 318 troops, he defeats the enemy forces and brings back all the plunder. To add to his virtue, he refuses the king of Sodom's tempting offer to share the plunder, lest anyone should think he was made rich by a godless king. He had made that mistake once before in Egypt (verses 22–24). It is a great and shining day for Abram. But in case we get ahead of ourselves and begin to imagine that Abram is the Lord's ultimate deliverer or Savior, the Lord does something thoroughly remarkable. He inserts into the situation a person who points us beyond Abram to a greater King to come.

> "...the king of Sodom went out to meet [Abram] at the Valley of Shaveh (that is, the King's Valley). And Melchizedek king of Salem brought out bread and wine. (He was priest of God Most High.) And he blessed him and said, 'Blessed be Abram by God Most High, Possessor of heaven and earth; and blessed be God Most High, who has delivered your enemies into your hand!' And Abram gave him a tenth of everything" (verses 17–20).

Melchizedek is one of the most intriguing figures in the Bible. He appears out of nowhere, but he is a figure of dignity and unique significance. Abram is meeting with the king of Sodom after he has helped bail him out at a place called the King's Valley. Another king by the name of Melchizedek (literally, "King of Righteousness") joins them. He is king of a place called "Salem," which means peace, and which sounds a lot like "Jeru-*salem*." So, we have a mysterious king named King of Righteousness and King of Peace appearing from nowhere. Added to that, we are told that he is priest of God Most High. In ancient Israel, you were either a priest or a king, but you were not both. In fact, kings were not allowed to get involved in priestly duties. This was off-limits. But this figure is both priest and king. He pronounces a blessing on Abram. The New Testament book of Hebrews tells us that means that Melchizedek is the superior one here, as the lesser person is blessed by the greater (Hebrews 7:7). Abram, for his part, gives him a tithe which, we discover later in the Old Testament, is only given to a true priest of God.

This is all very intriguing. But what does it all mean? Genesis 14 is a moment of glory for Abram. He appears to be all that God has purposed his Savior to be. But at this very point, we are given a model of the *true* Savior to come, one who is both priest and king, one who can pronounce God's blessing, and one to whom all honor is due. At Abram's moment of glory, Melchizedek points us to the One who will outshine him in every way. We do not meet Melchizedek again. He is mentioned but once more in the Old Testament. Yet he had a key role to play here.

It is interesting to follow the ups and downs of Abram's record. In chapter 12, he was in Egypt pretending that his wife was merely his sister to save his own skin. At that point we needed the reminder and reassurance that God's plans do not rest on this flawed and failing man. In that dark time, we would never have imagined that he might be a savior of the world.

But now in chapter 14, he looks like such a hero. The temptation is to think that he is the be-all and end-all of God's saving purposes. Yet just at that moment, there comes a signal from heaven that there is one greater than Abram, one of true worth who will not merely save Lot from his folly, but humanity from its sin. It is so good how, in his blessing on Abram, Melchizedek reminds him that it is God Most High who has delivered these enemies into his hand (verse 20). That was just the thing Abram needed to hear in his hour of triumph. We approach this from the other side of the cross, of course. The Savior has come. We know his name, and we have seen his salvation.

At the same time, the essential issues for us today are not unlike those we encounter here in Genesis 14. We see a great Christian leader, or a great servant of the Lord, and we can sometimes attribute an almost messianic identity to such a person. The great evangelist, the great church planter, the great missionary, the great leader who has helped us personally—it is easy to put such people on a pedestal. Given that tendency, how urgently we need the simple reminder that there is but one King, one Priest, one Savior: the King of Righteousness, the King of Peace, the Lord Jesus himself. He alone can save. Whether leaders disappoint us or remain heroes and role models for us, our eyes need to remain fixed on the one true Savior, the one true King. That is a place of safety for us.

It is interesting to consider just how Abram might have been feeling in verse 16. He was probably on a bit of a high. The adrenaline had been pumping. Victory was his. Honor and gratitude must have been flowing toward him. How gracious of God, at that very moment, to give him this powerful picture of the greater King and true Savior who is to come. If we have a moment or two of glory—perhaps we have served well, maybe there is appreciation for something we have done—we need a reminder that we are not the Savior. That job has been taken and that role has been fulfilled.

The final movement of Handel's *Messiah*, drawn from Revelation 5, always sends shivers down my spine with its sheer majesty:

> "Worthy is the Lamb that was slain…
> to receive power and riches, and wisdom, and strength,
> and honor, and glory, and blessing.
> Blessing and honor, glory and power be unto Him
> that sitteth upon the throne and unto the Lamb,
> For ever and ever and ever and ever…"

In this moment of triumph for a servant of God, Melchizedek comes as a pointer to the true King and Savior. The point is so simple: *he* alone is worthy to receive power and wealth and wisdom and might and honor and glory and blessing. *He* is the star of the show. The star is not Abram, great as he may be here. The star is not our particular hero of the faith, not our mentor. It is certainly not us. The great hero of the story, the true King and Savior, is none other than the Lord Jesus Christ. He alone is worthy, and he is the one to whom, alone, the glory is due.

4

Grace in times of fear

Genesis 15

Have you ever wondered whether the Lord will come through and whether things will turn out all right for you in the end, as you follow him? Maybe you have taken some great step of faith just lately or embraced some cost or risk to serve him. Your reputation, relationships, financial security—perhaps your *everything*—is on the line. Now you wonder whether God will leave you high and dry. You have faith but, if you are honest, it is a *fearful faith*. As we encounter Abram, the great man of faith, at the start of Genesis 15, we find that he is in a season in which he is sorely tempted to fearfulness.[1]

At the end of Genesis 14, Abram had acted with faith and valor. He was involved in rescuing the cities of Canaan from the kings of Mesopotamia. The king of Sodom had offered Abram a deal: *I will take the people; you take the spoils.* In response, Abram made a faith-filled and rather noble declaration:

> "I have lifted my hand to the Lord, God Most High, Possessor of heaven and earth, that I would not take a thread or a sandal strap or anything that is yours, lest you should say, 'I have made Abram rich'" (14:22–23).

I am not going to go down the road of wheeling and dealing with unbelieving kings and allowing myself to become beholden to any of them, least of all to the king of sin city, Sodom itself. No, thank you. I am going to rely on the Lord. You keep the spoils, the treasure; I will wait on the Lord. It was a stake in the ground for integrity, for faith, and for trusting the Lord.

We move forward just one verse, crossing the chapter divide into Genesis 15, and now see that the Lord knows what is on Abram's mind. Having made this grand declaration in a rush of adrenaline, Abram's pulse has now settled down a bit, and fear threatens to seep into his heart. Unwelcome, intrusive thoughts come into his mind: *What if the Lord now allows me to miss out? I just forsook considerable wealth and spoils. I signed away a big fortune. Now that I am back from the battle and sitting at home in the deafening silence on my own, some realities are dawning on me. To be quite honest, I am feeling a little unsettled. What if I have made a big mistake? What if I miss out?* Abram does persevere in faith, as we will see. He does not entertain those thoughts for long. But the Lord knows that they are not far from his mind.[2] In that moment when Abram is tempted to fear, the Lord brings his word to him in a powerful vision: "Fear not, Abram, I am your shield; your reward shall be very great" (verse 1). *Abram, you have made some sacrifices. You may be feeling nervous about how things are going to work out. But do not fear. In trusting me, you have made the right call. I am your defense and your shield. The reward that will come to you is very great.*

In Abram's reply, we get to the root of the issue:

> "But Abram said, 'O Lord God, what will you give me, for I continue childless, and the heir of my house is Eliezer of Damascus?... Behold, you have given me no offspring, and a member of my household will be my heir'" (verses 2–3).

It is wonderfully honest. He remains respectful as a man of faith and he opens his question appropriately, "O LORD God..."[3] But Abram is not hiding the contents of his heart: *You have just said that my reward will be great. But this whole idea that I am going to have a nation's worth of grandchildren is not looking too likely. We do not have any kids. We are both old and getting older. Sarai is still barren. In fact, I have gone ahead and made a member of my household my heir: Eliezer of Damascus. Lord, I am finding it hard not to fear that you are going to let me down at this point. That is the truth. I have walked by faith. I have said no to some of the enticements of this world. You have been faithful, but the future threatens to unsettle me. The uncertainty is hard. As I look out on the days ahead, the picture is frankly a little bleak.*

Does that sound familiar in any way for you? Have you ever been there? Maybe you are there right now. We all know something of living through seasons where we are sorely tempted to weaken in faith and to fall into fear. For some of us, it goes beyond temptation. We become gripped by fear, even as we struggle to hold to faith. For servants tempted to fear and grappling with fear—particularly for those currently gripped by fear—the Lord brings powerful reassurance and deep grace. This reassurance and grace extend through Abram to us, as we seek to walk by faith in our day. Notice what the Lord brings to the believer in fearful times.

The help of a powerful visual aid

The other evening, it was cool and crisp and clear. Not a cloud in the sky. I was out with the kids, throwing a football around at dusk, and the stars were starting to really come to life in the darkening sky. Before we turned in, we went to the far end of our back yard, far away from the lights of the house and street. We lay down on the grass and just looked up at the canopy of stars. It was breathtaking.

In response to Abram's probing, "What will you give me?", the Lord puts his arm round him, as it were, brings him outside and says: "Look toward heaven, and number the stars, if you are able to number them" (verse 5). *Just look at that night sky. Try to begin to count the stars.* Of course, he could not count them. The Lord said to Abram, very simply: "So shall your offspring be" (verse 5). The stars are impossible to count, numerous beyond number. The promises of God look so unlikely. Abram is old, Sarai is barren. There were no children on the horizon. But the Lord reaffirms his promise and gives Abram a reminder that will be his to hold onto, a visual aid that will speak to him of the promise each and every evening as he sits outside his tent with his cup of cocoa, chatting to Sarai at the end of the day. There are still no children, there is still no progress, but the sky itself is the canvas on which is painted his reminder of the faithfulness of God. Hundreds of stars, thousands of stars, millions of stars. The Lord has not forgotten his promise and he will not fail.

Was this reminder just for Abram? Are we simply to look over his shoulder and observe from afar? The New Testament tells us that all who share the faith of Abram are his descendants. We are part of his family, not necessarily ethnically or biologically, but members of the family of faith. If we are believers, we are children of Abram in that sense. Think about the promise. God knew that the blessing of Abram, given to him in Genesis 12, would stretch beyond his physical descendants to his spiritual descendants as well, to the church of Jesus Christ. And this visual aid points to that spiritual reality. Reflecting on that, the power of that picture suddenly hits home. God makes it so clear through his Word that his intention has always been to create an enormous global people of faith. The wonderful vision of the saints of Revelation 9–10 comes to mind:

> "After this I looked, and behold, a great multitude that no one could number, from every nation, from all tribes and peoples and languages, standing before the throne and before the Lamb, clothed in white robes, with palm branches in their hands, and crying out with a loud voice, 'Salvation belongs to our God who sits on the throne and to the Lamb!'"

The picture of the stars in that ancient near eastern sky all those years ago points to the glorious company of the redeemed family of God. They are from every nation and tribe and people and tongue, and too numerous to count. That is where this story is going. Recognizing that, the visual aid given as a comfort and reassurance to Abram that starry night comes to us with the same force of comfort and reassurance. We look out on a chaotic and needy world, on a broken and lost society, on our conflicted and hostile culture, and we can wonder if those around us will ever come to saving faith in Jesus. Is there any real hope for the church of Christ to be built?

The obstacles are huge, and the opposition is real. Faith can quickly turn to fear, and even to despair. But the Word of God points our eyes to a real-time visual aid. It points our eyes to the night sky and reminds us that God promised to Abram a great big global family—a family, not only of physical descendants, but of spiritual descendants too. And God is not done; his purpose is not yet finished. The family will continue to grow beyond all counting. It is a majestic thought. Looking up at the night sky lifts us out of our context to contemplate something big and grand and glorious and cosmic. It reminds us of our Creator and his power. It transcends the ups and downs of human history. It transcends the rise and fall of governments and movements, of cultures and civilizations. It points us to the power of the eternal God of heaven and earth to achieve his plans and his purposes, in his time and in his way. It reminds us that this great God will grow his family and build his church, and that nothing will stop him.

In fearful days such as ours, this is a great encouragement. It is worth taking a moment to go out and look at the night sky. We should praise and thank God that his promises will not fail and that his family of redeemed children will continue to grow beyond number, despite all obstacles along the way.

The gift of righteousness

There are occasions where a brief statement is put in such a simple and unadorned way that we can almost overlook its weight and significance. A survivor of the Holocaust describes the experience of American soldiers driving their tank through the gates of the concentration camp where he was due to be killed and simply shouting, "You're free."[4] Two simple words, but bearing such incredible significance, and full of such joyful hope. You can imagine the prisoners wondering if they misheard it. *Did the soldiers really say that? Did they mean it? Is it true?*

Genesis 15:6 is one of the weightiest and most hope-filled verses in all the Bible. It is a profound statement of the basic principle underlying the gospel. It points forward to the work of Christ and the key divine mechanism of salvation. It is foundational to New Testament faith. Yet it is put so simply. We could easily read the chapter and skim over it. In the face of Abram's questions and his grappling with fear, God has reaffirmed his promise to give Abram a great family of descendants. In response to God's promise, we read: "And he believed the LORD, and he counted it to him as righteousness" (verse 6). To be righteous is to be "right" with God, a declaration by God the Judge that you are innocent and that all is well with you in his divine courtroom. We know full well that Abram did not have a perfectly righteous record. Far from it. We only need look back to chapter 12 to see a major moral lapse in his behavior and we only need to look forward to chapter 16 to see another one.

As we zoom out from Abram and his story, we see quickly and clearly that no one has a perfectly righteous record. This has been the heart of the human problem ever since Adam and Eve rebelled against God in the Garden. It is why humanity is stuck outside the Garden. It is why suffering and death have come into the world. Those things are the judgment of God for our failure to be and do what is right in his sight. Despite all this, God had set Abram apart and promised to bring salvation blessings to him, his family and to the nations of the world through him. The great promise of Genesis 12 raises fundamental questions: What about human rebellion? What about the fact of humanity's guilt before God? How will salvation blessings come when the problem of sin remains?

Here in verse 6, in just a dozen or so English words, we get the heart of the answer. Abram is given a reaffirmation of God's promise. He is called upon to believe and trust what God says. And we read: "he believed the LORD, and he counted it to him as righteousness." We tend to assume that if there is a God whom we will meet at the end of our lives, he will either accept or reject us based on how we have lived our lives. Yet look what God the Judge does here with Abram. It is so remarkable, so striking, so surprising. He looks on Abram's faith-response to his word, faltering and fearful though it is, and he "counts" that faith to Abram as righteousness. He *reckons* it to him. As Abram believes his word, God the Judge decides to credit to Abram's account a full measure of perfect righteousness.

God is not saying: *Abram, I am so impressed that you believe my promise. I want you to know that this cancels out all the wrong things you have done, and this makes you fit and ready for heaven. You have earned it, my friend!* Not at all. This declaration or transfer is not achieved by Abram's faith as an act of merit or because of something he has done. We must not misread this and think Abram *earned* the righteousness he received in verse 6.

Imagine getting a letter from your bank with a spectacular offer. They are offering to pay off the balance of your mortgage—$100,000, $200,000, all of it! They will cancel the loan completely and all you need to do in return is to fill out a response form and give your signature in acceptance. Amazing. Would it were true! In this scenario, there is no equivalence between what you need to do and what the bank is offering: a response form compared to a gift of hundreds of dollars. That is the kind of thing that is going on here in Genesis. Abram's belief does not *buy* him a not-guilty verdict. Signing a bank form could never *earn* the discharge of your mortgage. In this imaginary—and frankly unbelievable—scenario, the reason you get your mortgage paid off is because you take the bank at their word and accept their offer. Here in Genesis 15, God shows Abram, and us, that he will give the gift of righteousness to those who take him at his word, incredible as it may seem. He will give the gift of a not-guilty verdict to all who believe that his promises are true. This is how God's salvation blessings will come. We do not know the details yet. We do not actually know the "account" from which this great store of righteousness will be drawn at this point in the Bible story. But the principle—and it is a breathtaking one—is that God will not save us based on our good works or our own moral record. We would never be saved if that were the case. No, our God counts righteousness to unrighteous people *who take him at his word*, who have faith.

The apostle Paul devotes almost an entire chapter of his great letter to the Romans to this verse. In Romans 4, he explains how this key verse from Genesis 15 teaches us that our salvation comes as a *gift*, and not as a payment for our good works. He insists that these words speak to us directly:

> "But the words 'it was counted to him' were not written for his sake alone, but for ours also. It will be counted to us who believe in him who raised from the dead Jesus our Lord, who was delivered up for our trespasses and raised for our justification" (Romans 4:23–25).

Those words were written for us, to teach us that righteousness is counted to us when we believe in the God who gave his Son for our sin, and who raised him to life for our justification. This is the heart of everything. This is the fundamental principle of the faith and the core of the gospel.

I want to emphasize this because it is so important. I want to emphasize it in case there are those reading who imagine they do not need what Abram needed—the gift of righteousness. Maybe that is you. Maybe you do not have a sense of spiritual need or of guilt before God. Great Abram, the father of the people of Israel, *needed* God to credit to him a righteousness that was not his own. This hero of faith needed forgiveness. This is your fundamental need, and it is mine as well. Others may be at the other end of the spectrum. Maybe you carry the burden of knowing full well that you have not met God's requirements. You know you have not lived up to his standards, and you are laboring under a sense of obligation to *do* everything you can to make yourself right before him and to earn his favor. If that is you, may I urge you to stop? Look at verse 6: God credits righteousness *to the unrighteous*. He gives it as a gift to *all who believe*. Have you received that gift? If you have, will you rest today in the security and the peace of it, knowing that God the Judge counts you righteous in his sight?

The security of the covenant

In fearful times, God has given his servant Abram the help of a powerful visual aid and promised him the gift of righteousness. At this point in the narrative, God reminds him that he is the God who has shown deliverance in the past and who intends to show his faithfulness in the future. "I am the LORD who brought you out from Ur of the Chaldeans to give you this land to possess" (verse 7). That is a steadying reminder of who God is and what he intends to do. However, Abram is still feeling a little shaky and needing reassurance. "But [Abram] said, "O Lord GOD, how am I to know that I shall possess it?" (verse 8). *Where is the evidence for me? Where is the proof?* It seems surprising to us that this man of faith should be pressing God like this. Yet God does not turn a deaf ear to his request, but gives him profound assurance.

I recently saw famous footage showing the signing of the agreement between Germany and the Allied Forces that brought the Second World War to an end. In a sense, the whole world held its breath as the ink soaked into the paper on that day. Throughout much of human history, nations have related to one another on the basis of formal treaties. In the ancient world of Abram's day, important agreements were sealed and established in ceremonies rather like the one we see here. It all looks strange to us. God calls upon Abram to bring to him "a heifer three years old, a female goat three years old, a ram three years old, a turtledove, and a young pigeon" (verse 9). The animals (but not the birds) are then cut in two and each half is separated. This kind of covenant ceremony was evidently known to the ancient world. The parties entering into the covenant would walk between the pieces of the slain animals. The implication of that act would be this: *If either of us breaks the terms of this covenant, or contract, we will accept the fate of these animals for ourselves. We recognize that the penalty for breaching the covenant is death. Our very lives are on the line.* You get just a glimmer of this when you sign a mortgage or a lease agreement. If you read through the fine print, you know that the penalties you are risking in entering into the covenant are huge. If you do not make your payments, you lose your home. If you back out of the agreement early, you may face penalties of crippling sums of money.

In this type of covenant in Genesis, the very lives of the two parties are on the line. That seems to be the symbolic meaning of the slaughtered animals. But how things proceed from here is far from normal. As the sun sets on this rather dramatic scene, one of the two parties in the covenant falls into a deep sleep and a "dreadful and great darkness" falls upon him (verse 12). This hardly looks as though it is going to be an equal partnership. One signatory to the covenant is out for the count. If you fell asleep in the bank manager's office when signing a mortgage agreement, the manager might gingerly remove the papers and quickly shred them, for fear of taking on risk with a client of poor health or limited strength. However, as Abram sleeps, the Lord then speaks to him, promising him both trouble and triumph in the years to come. Now the scene gets even more strange and dramatic. "When the sun had gone down and it was dark, behold, a smoking fire pot and a flaming torch passed between the pieces" (verse 17). On more than one occasion in Scripture, fire is a physical manifestation of the presence of God. Here Abram is being shown that God's own presence is passing between these rows of slaughtered animals. While Abram lies in a daze from his deep sleep, God himself enters into the covenant obligation. As he does so, he reaffirms his covenant commitment to give the land of promise to Abram and his family.

What is all this telling Abram and what is it teaching us? The symbolism is as powerful as it is profound. God has entered into a covenant with his chosen people. Remarkably, in entering into this covenant, God is taking upon himself the cost and responsibility of it. He is saying that if the covenant is broken, he will bear the risk and even the penalty. The Old Testament is full of vivid pictures that point us forward to the cross of Calvary. This is one of the most striking and most wonderful of all. Should the covenant be broken, God himself is committing to pay the cost—even the cost of death itself. God is the God of faithfulness. He will never break the covenant. But Abram and his children, both physical and spiritual, are not given to faithfulness. The people of God will fail again and again to meet the requirements of the covenant and to live in faithfulness. Who will pay the breakage clause, the penalties for infraction? Who will bear the curse of death itself? Not Abram, not his people, not me, and not you; God himself will, in the Person of his Son. He will bear it for all those who are part of the covenant by faith. As the divine presence passed between those slain animal parts, there is a foreshadowing of another journey that God will take: the journey of the Son of God, Jesus Christ, as he carries his cross to Calvary and dies so that the people of the covenant may live.

When we find ourselves wondering if God will come through for us, if he will keep his promises and do us good, here is the deepest and most profound comfort and reassurance. It is found in this biblical image of God taking the walk of the covenant on his own between these slain animal parts in Genesis 15, and then in the image of the Son of God taking the walk of the covenant to the hill of Calvary thousands of years later.[5] For those of fearful faith, the greatest comfort of all is the comfort that God has taken upon himself the full cost of the covenant that we might be secure within it, despite all our sin and failure and sheer unworthiness. And in those seasons of fear, we must look to Calvary. When things look most bleak and it seems as though God might not come through and might abandon us at the last, when we are in our darker moments, we look to the One who gave his life to make and keep his covenant with us. Our great comfort comes from knowing that the One who did such a thing *cannot* fail us, and *will never* fail us, in all the days that are to come.

5

The cost of self-reliance

Genesis 16

Does it ever seem to you that God's plans and purposes—his purposes for the gospel, the church, the world, or for you personally—are slow in coming to fruition? Gospel progress is sometimes slow. Reaching the unreached, to the ends of the earth, takes time and we might ask whether the job will ever get done. You may sense that the Lord has given you a certain task or responsibility, but it is hard to gain traction. You have it on your heart to serve in a particular way, but the opportunity has not presented itself. You may feel it is his will for you to marry, but it has not happened yet. You believe he wants you to pray for a relative to come to faith, and you have prayed for years, but there has been no change.

When we are called to wait for the outworking of God's plans and purposes, a great temptation can often arise. It is the temptation to take matters into our own hands and seek to achieve God's purposes in our own way, in our own time, and on our own terms. Genesis 16 is the story of two servants of God, both people of faith, who succumb to that temptation. It is a messy incident and a blot on their record to be sure. It comes to us as a cautionary tale. It is a warning against taking matters into our own hands. At the same time, it highlights the sheer grace of God whose plans and purposes will not be derailed or destroyed by the folly of his servants.

It highlights the domino effect of sin

Genesis 16 is a story of two believers who attempt to pursue God's will in humanity's way, and it highlights the domino effect of sin. The journey of faith has been a bit of a rollercoaster for Abram and Sarai thus far. There have been real highs, where they have trusted God and walked with him in costly obedience, responding to his word of promise. There have been some lows; times of fear and outright failure. In the grand sweep of their story, chapter 16 marks a particular low. It reads like a Greek tragedy and, as the drama unfolds, it makes you wince. Maybe you have watched a film or read a novel like this where the key characters walk headlong into a disaster, and you want to cry out and warn them to stop. Each new move and compromise digs them into a deeper hole.

The chapter opens on an ominous note: "Now Sarai, Abram's wife, had borne him no children" (verse 1). Given what we know of God's promise to make a great nation of this family, this is a real problem. Only a few verses before, God had taken Abram outside to look at the night sky and had told him that his offspring would number as many as the stars. He had confirmed the covenant in a dramatic ceremony. At the end of chapter 15, the promises of God were ringing in Abram's ears. But the hard reality was that Abram and Sarai were old and getting older, and Sarai was still barren. They had been living in Canaan for a decade (verse 3), and Abram was in his mid-80s (verse 16). It must have been incredibly tough for Sarai emotionally and spiritually. The hopes and expectations of the family—in fact, the promises of God for the future—rested on her having a baby. And it simply was not happening. She and Abram were people of faith. They had not drifted into agnosticism or atheism. They were not on the verge of giving up on the God of the covenant. But Sarai evidently could not see how the great promises of God were going to be fulfilled unless she and Abram did something, and something drastic.

An idea occurs to her. It was not unheard of in the ancient world for servants to bear children in place of their mistress if she was unable to conceive. Sarai looks at her Egyptian servant, Hagar, and sees an uncomfortable but efficient solution to a seemingly impossible problem. She puts the idea to Abram: "And Sarai said to Abram, 'Behold now, the LORD has prevented me from bearing children. Go in to my servant; it may be that I shall obtain children by her'" (verse 2).

Often when you hear about a major disaster, it becomes clear that there had been a series of bad moves by a series of people, creating a perfect storm or a domino effect. A nuclear reactor overheats because of a problem in engineering, and another problem in manufacture, followed by a problem in monitoring and control, then an extra element of human error. A ship sinks because of a design flaw compounded by a loading imbalance, made dangerous through a navigation error during bad weather. It all comes together to make for a terrible disaster. Here in Genesis 16, we begin to see the domino effect of a series of sinful blunders.

This first one, on the part of Sarai, is such a warning to us. She is not intending to turn her back on the Lord. She is not questioning God's existence or his plan, nor is she converting to a pagan religion. She has just grown weary of waiting. In her impatience, she has decided that it is time to take things into her own hands. *God does not seem to be doing it; I will help him out and make it happen myself.* It was not out of step with the culture of the time, but it simply is not God's way. Nowhere has God said that polygamy is his plan. Nowhere did he invite Abram and Sarai to consider this as an option. The first domino falls in the heart and mind of Sarai as she decides to take things into her own hands.

The next one comes right away, and this time, it is Abram who takes a wrong turn. Sarai tells Abram about her plan and "Abram listened to the voice of Sarai" (verse 2). Within a marriage, God gives a husband and a wife to one another to provide counsel and encouragement. In particular, the husband has a role of giving godly leadership. But Abram does not counterbalance Sarai's suggestion by speaking sense and wisdom into the situation. He just hears the heartache in her voice and the urgency of her appeal and goes along with the plan unquestioningly. He completely abdicates his responsibility of leadership and ducks the opportunity to steer things in a godly and faithful direction. It is an echo of what happened in the Garden of Eden where the serpent spoke words of temptation to Eve, she was taken in, and Adam followed her in her sin, without raising a single question or objection.

Another domino falls and the plan is initiated: "So, after Abram had lived ten years in the land of Canaan, Sarai, Abram's wife, took Hagar the Egyptian, her servant, and gave her to Abram her husband as a wife" (verse 3). The mess gets messier. Abram goes along with the plan he should have lovingly and firmly refused, abandons his monogamous commitment to Sarai and embraces the polygamy of the surrounding cultures. This plan, this sin, opens the door to more sin. The next domino quickly falls. Hagar duly becomes pregnant, and "when she saw that she had conceived, she looked with contempt on her mistress" (verse 4).

It is hard to imagine all Hagar's emotions in this, how she might have felt in being asked or coerced or even forced into this arrangement. We simply are not told. But once she conceives, we see a little of what she is feeling as she looks with contempt on her childless mistress. Respect for Sarai, which would have been fitting within the household, gives way to smugness and contempt. Now Hagar is a wife of Abram like Sarai is, but she has the upper hand because she has produced an heir. Sarai feels hurt and humiliated, and another domino falls as she turns her anger on Abram: "May the wrong done to me be on you! I gave my servant to your embrace, and when she saw that she had conceived, she looked on me with contempt. May the LORD judge between you and me!" (verse 5). *It is all your fault, Abram. I let you marry my servant to help the situation move forward, but look what has happened. The Lord will judge but I know the verdict: you are guilty. It's all on you.*

We do not want to be too hard on Sarai here in her distress, but we must acknowledge how unreasonable this seems. She wanted it this way, and it was never going to be easy. The situation has now led to tension and acrimony between Sarai and Abram. Things quickly get worse. Abram does not attempt to speak reason into the situation; there is no gentle rebuttal to the tirade. He just redirects Sarai's anger to the fundamentally helpless Hagar: "Behold, your servant is in your power; do to her as you please" (verse 6). *Look, Hagar may be my wife now, but she came into this house as* your *servant. Do to her whatever you want.* The terrible behavior continues to stack up. Abram totally fails to acknowledge that Hagar needs protection even though she was dragged into the situation, her freedom and dignity trampled underfoot. Now Abram allows her to become a whipping post for Sarai's anger.

It is not long before the next domino falls. Sarai does what we anticipate she would and deals harshly with her former servant. She deepens her own sin and shame by abusing a defenseless woman in her household. And all this leads to the falling of yet another domino. The unhappy Hagar flees.

She runs for it. We can hardly fault her for that. But it is a sad outcome because, despite everything, the blessing of God rests upon Abram's family and household. Ultimately, for Hagar to know the salvation blessings of God, she needs to remain part of the family of faith, however messy that family is. One domino after another, after another. The initial inclination to take matters into human hands sets off a cascade of other sins and their effects. Sin begets sin here. Things go from bad to worse. The domino effect in this tragic drama is a warning to us in those seasons when the plans of God for the gospel, the church, for our loved ones, and for us personally seem slow to come to fruition. It is a warning whenever we are tempted to take matters into our own hands and to drive them forward in our own way.

Maybe you have experienced this kind of temptation in the midst of a ministry endeavor. Things are not coming together as you expected or planned; the Lord has not provided as you had anticipated; he has not brought partners or opened doors; but you are determined anyway. Or maybe you have seen it in your own evangelism or discipleship of loved ones. The Lord has not done a work in their heart that you long that he would do, so you push and cajole—and the results are not pretty. Or maybe it is in your personal life. The Lord has not provided the believing spouse you have been praying for, and you think to yourself: *If he will not come through for me, I will find a sympathetic non-Christian, and I will make it work.* Of course, the results are messy. Whatever the specific details, this is a real yet subtle temptation and danger for us who know the Lord. Abram and Sarai were not saying they did not have faith that God's promises were true. They were not walking away from the Lord or stopping serving him. They believed God's promises were true and that his plans would come to fruition, but they wrongly assumed that if God seemed slow in working out his purposes, it was right for them to take matters into their own hands. They thought it was fine for them to employ an efficient shortcut and drive things forward by human means. But one sin led to another, and another, and another—and there was carnage at every turn. Pursuing God's plans humanity's way simply highlighted the domino effect of sin.

It highlights the abundant grace of God

In the midst of this messy story, we also see God pouring out his grace on everyone, the first of whom is Hagar. It is hard to imagine Hagar's feelings at this moment. She has been used and abused. Now she is a homeless single mother fleeing from a painful and oppressive situation, alone in the wilderness. We can only imagine the weight of her heart and the anxiety of her mind. *How will all this play out? What will happen next? Is there any hope for me?* Verse 7 is quite lovely: "The angel of the LORD found her by a spring of water in the wilderness, the spring on the way to Shur."

This is the first time in the Bible where we encounter the "angel of the LORD." This figure occasionally appears at key moments in the life of God's people. He is somewhat mysterious to us. He is not simply an ordinary angel. Those who meet with the angel of the Lord feel that they have met with the Lord himself and have heard his voice. That is what Hagar feels from what we read in verse 13. We may well ask: Is this the Lord himself? Is this a pre-incarnate visitation from the Second Person of the Trinity, as many have suggested? We do not know for certain. The Scriptures do not address all our speculations, but we do know that in the person of the angel of the Lord, the Lord comes to Hagar in a special way in the wilderness. He asks her where she has come from and where she is going. He knows the answer, of course. She is fleeing from Sarai. In response, he gives to her an instruction and a promise:

> "The angel of the LORD said to her, 'Return to your mistress and submit to her.' The angel of the LORD also said to her, 'I will surely multiply your offspring so that they cannot be numbered for multitude'" (verses 9–10).

It might sound tough that the Lord sends Hagar back to Abram's house, but the blessing of God was on the household of Abram. Going back to the family of promise was to go back to the place of blessing. Hagar needed the protection and provision of a home. So, the Lord tells her to go back. With that instruction comes a great promise: Hagar is going to be the matriarch of a very great family. This outcast slave woman will have innumerable children of her own, so many "that they cannot be numbered for multitude." The promise has echoes of the promise to Abram, which itself is not surprising. This child will not be *the child* through whom all the promises of God will come. Nonetheless, this son of Abram will be the father of a huge family. He shall be called Ishmael and his name will have a deep significance. Rather wonderfully, the angel of the Lord breaks out into poetry here. That is why the format of the text changes:

> "Behold, you are pregnant and shall bear a son. You shall call his name Ishmael, because the LORD has listened to your affliction" (verse 11).

Often in the Bible when a baby is coming or a child is born, there are words of poetic celebration. Even a baby who comes amid trying circumstances comes as a gift and is a cause for celebration. That is still true today, of course. The name Ishmael means "God hears." "You shall call his name Ishmael, because the LORD has listened to your affliction." How reassuring and good. God has heard. This child's name is going to be the symbolic significance of his life. His mother was a slave within a household where she was placed in an impossible and abusive situation. She was powerless and had to flee. She was pregnant and alone. She had nowhere to turn. It is a tragic story that has been repeated in one form or other far too often. We can imagine Hagar weeping and despairing by that spring of water in the wilderness. She probably thought that no one would hear her cries or care about her heartache, yet the Lord came to her with the message: *I have heard your cries. I have heard you in your distress. I am the God who hears.*

Hagar got the message:

> "So she called the name of the LORD who spoke to her, 'You are a God of seeing,' for she said, 'Truly here I have seen him who looks after me.' Therefore, the well was called Beer-lahai-roi [which means the well of the Living One who sees me]" (verses 13–14).

God is the God who hears, when perhaps no one else is listening. God is the God who sees, when perhaps no one else notices. In a messy situation where plenty of sin and foolishness made bad things get a lot worse very quickly, we see the grace of God. In a story where the weak and marginalized come off the worst, as they usually do, God hears the cry of the unheard one. He sees the distress of the unseen one. It is not that Hagar was sinlessly innocent in all this. She has been terribly wronged and she herself has done wrong. But the Lord's grace meets her in her time of need.

I wonder if you have been pushed into a distressing situation, or got yourself into one, through a complex mixture of your sin and the sin of others. Maybe you feel helpless and alone. You cry out in distress, but wonder if anyone *hears*. You may be suffering and in need, but wonder if anyone *sees*. You may resonate with

Hagar's wilderness experience because the wilderness is precisely where you feel you are today. If that is you, here is what you need to know about the God of the Bible: he is the God of grace. He is the God who hears the cries of the distressed. He is the God who sees the one who weeps.

Consider as well how his grace is extended to Sarai and Abram, who really did make a mess of things in this saga. Genesis 16 is a major "down" in their rollercoaster story. It is a dramatic dip. By any measure of reasonableness, God could well have given up on them at this point. They are a bit of a disaster, after all. They are not waiting on God as they should. They are not honoring their marriage as they should. Their behavior toward Hagar hardly covers them in glory.

And yet. *And yet...* God is going to reaffirm his covenant with Abram in the very next chapter. He will proceed with his plan to bless Abram and his family, and through them, the world. In fact, when we get to the New Testament and the writers there look back on Abram and Sarai, they focus on the fact that this couple were people of faith who walked by faith. Have Paul and the writer of Hebrews not read Genesis 16? Have they not seen what happened here? Of course, they have. They know the failures. But the story is all bracketed by and covered with the grace of God. He takes a sinful couple and their messy story and he bears with them. He takes flawed servants of faltering faith and walks with them. He continues to use them, and, at the end of the day, he calls them people of faith. He calls them his own people. What an encouragement that is for us today who are likewise flawed and sinful people of faltering faith. What an encouragement it is that God does not give up on his failing servants or cast them off because of their sin. Despite all the ways in which we fail him as people of faith, we have hope that he will continue to show us his abundant grace.

It highlights the choice between two ways to live

In Galatians 4, the apostle Paul reflects on the saga of Hagar and Sarah and their sons. He points out how it illustrates two approaches to life, two ways of relating to God himself.

> "For it is written that Abraham had two sons, one by a slave woman and one by a free woman. But the son of the slave was born according to the flesh, while the son of the free woman was born through promise" (Galatians 4:22–23).

The story of Hagar's son Ishmael and Sarai's son Isaac points to two very different ways to live. One is the way of the flesh, humanity's way; and the other is the way of the promise. Ishmael was born because Abram and Sarai decided to take matters into their own hands, find their own solution, and deal with things in their own way. It was very human, very fleshly. Isaac, by contrast, would be born on God's terms, through his own miraculous work and in accordance with his own promise. Paul wants us to see that these two children symbolize two very different ways to approach God and to live before him. One is the do-it-yourself approach, and the other is the trust-in-the-promise approach.

The other day, my car went to the carwash for the first time in a long while. The place I went is a sort of car washing emporium. As you drive in, there are two options. You can veer left and head for the large do-it-yourself area, where you drive into a bay with all the equipment you need to wash your car. You put on your wellington boots and rain gear and get thoroughly involved in the process. Or, you can veer right and have the machine do it all for you. You line up the wheels in the track without grinding your rims—no small challenge for some of us—kick the car into neutral and let yourself be wafted along through the suds and the spray and the wheel buffers while everything is done for you.

At the end of the day, there are only two religions in the world, two ways to approach God, two ways to live: the self-serve approach, where you try to get things done your way and on your terms, and the approach where you allow God to take care of things. One is the way of *effort*, the other is the way of *belief*. One is the way of *works*, the other is the way of *faith*. Ishmael was born through the former approach. Abram and Sarai reckoned they had to figure things out for themselves. Isaac would be born because of God's sole initiative and power. He would fulfill his promise against all human odds, doing all that was necessary himself.

It is fundamental to genuine faith that we learn to take God at his word and leave things in his hands. We all need to learn, and then remember, that vital lesson. Many of us already believe that we are justified by faith and not by works. We know salvation comes through believing the promises of God and not by anything we do. But having been saved by faith, we easily imagine that we live the Christian life by our own efforts or ingenuity. Once we are into the kingdom, we think it is now down to us to make a go of things. But if we think that way, we run the risk of making the same mistake as Abram and Sarai. The truth is that we who are saved by faith must *go on living by faith* each and every day. The way we begin the Christian life is the way in which we must continue in the Christian life. Where are you in danger of taking matters into your own hands? Where are you in danger of engaging in a do-it-yourself religion, doing things the human way, rather than simply trusting the promises of God and waiting upon him to work things out in his way, in his time, by his powerful means? Let me urge you, as I urge myself: Trust him today. Let him work out his plans in his way, and just see what he might do.

6

The sign of the covenant

Genesis 17

We live in the supreme age of the consumer. Never before have we had so much choice available to us or so much advertising vying for our attention. We are, by cultural identity and historical peculiarity, *consumers par excellence*. A leading market research firm has analyzed the different eras over the last century. According to their analysis, 1900–1960 was the age of manufacturing; 1960–1990 was the age of distribution; 1990–2010 was the age of information; and since 2010, we have been living in *the age of the consumer*. Dominance in the marketplace comes from "engaging with empowered consumers," and the consumer reigns supreme.[1] In the world's great marketplace of religions and ideas, so many people circulate from stall to stall, examining the products as empowered shoppers seeking the best, most attractive deal. We wonder which religion will be privileged to have our involvement. We come expecting to receive rather than to give, and certainly not willing to commit.

As society has taught us, we come as consumers, interested to know what the Lord will do for us, interested to discover what gifts are on offer. Eternal life? The free offer of forgiveness? A warm welcome to a new family? A loving Father? These perks sound good. But when we hear about the call of Jesus to live a transformed life, to give, to serve, to be set apart and distinct form those around us, we quickly close our ears. We dip in for the sermon on Sunday, perhaps, but slip away before real demands can be placed upon us. Whether that profile fits us personally or not, we all have to admit that the idea of commitment-free faith appeals.

Genesis 17 cuts right through our consumer mentality and shows us that the Lord who freely gives salvation also demands of us all that we are and have. Whenever we function as consumers—buying a new home or car or choosing the right vacation or insurance policy—we feel we are in the position of power. And in a sense, we are. The money is in our pocket. And when we circulate around the marketplace of religion, deciding which deity attracts our interest, we can easily imagine that the power resides with us. But Genesis 17 is here to teach us that God Almighty calls the shots and reigns supreme.

It is no mistake that at the start of this chapter the Lord refers to himself as "God Almighty." In fact, he *reintroduces* himself to Abram using that name: "When Abram was ninety-nine years old the Lord appeared to Abram and said to him, 'I am God Almighty; walk before me, and be blameless'" (verse 1). Throughout Genesis 17, the Almighty God dismantles and destroys our consumer mindset.

God establishes the timeline for his covenant work

One of the ways in which we seek to control our lives is by deciding the timescale for our plans. We will live in this house for five years; I will stay in this job ten years; we will go on that vacation in two years' time. I will take the car in for its service on the fifteenth; I can give you 30 minutes for that meeting next Wednesday at 2pm. Managing our time and our calendars is one of the chief ways we gain and maintain control in life. One of the fundamental lessons of Scripture, repeated again and again in different ways, is the simple but profound lesson that it is the Lord's prerogative to set the timeline for his plans and purposes. Our role is to wait upon him. Over time, we discover that, very often, *he really does call us to wait.* We are often in a rush; but God never is.

At this point in Abram's story, we are meant to take notice of the timeline. At the beginning of chapter 17 we are in Abram's one hundredth year: "When Abram was ninety-nine years old the LORD appeared to Abram and said…" The passage of time is important in this story. Abram's age matters here. Despite God's promises, Sarai remains barren and the biological clock continues to tick loudly throughout their story.

The Lord was not going to accept Abram and Sarai's Genesis 16 scheme as the means by which his plans would be fulfilled. *He* would bring about his promises. But just notice the action God takes. He actually does nothing for thirteen whole years that is recorded for us, not a single thing. That is the passage of time represented by the little white space in our Bible between the end of chapter 16 and the beginning of chapter 17. Abram and Sarai make this mess, take matters into their own hands and think they have found a way forward through their own scheming. God simply leaves them to wait for his next move. As far as we know, the Lord does nothing to intervene in this situation for thirteen whole years until Abram is 99 years old and Sarai is 90. What is the Lord doing here? Why the wait? He is showing his slow-to-learn servants that the timing is *his*, that their calendar belongs to *him*, and that the outworking of his plans and purposes will happen as and when *he* deems.

This is one of the very hardest lessons of faith for us to learn. The Lord has to keep teaching it to us. He has been teaching his people this lesson for thousands of years. From a human perspective, the salvation purposes of God in the Old Testament moved slowly. The people of Israel were in Egypt for 400 years. The journey through the wilderness took 40 years. The people of Judah spent 70 years in Babylon. The Old Testament era closed with 400 years of prophetic silence. The Messiah would take millennia to arrive. And the Lord was teaching his people through this. In the church today, progress in the work of the kingdom seems slow. Getting the gospel out to the ends of the earth is a painstaking process. As we wait for the Lord Jesus to return, we see culture deteriorate, the fabric of our society unfurl, and the laws of the land turn progressively against the Word of God. We see believers suffer and the world darken as the years pass, yet still the Savior has not returned. It feels like a long wait.

We pray fervently for personal spiritual growth, for the salvation of loved ones, for God's purposes in our lives to move forward—we pray and we wait. The wait can seem agonizingly long. Sometimes we live in that gap, in that white space between chapter 16 and chapter 17, with nothing happening and no new word from the Lord. It can be a very hard place to live. Perhaps you are living there today, waiting for the Lord, longing for him to act, crying out for him to intervene and move things forward. He is teaching you to wait. The lesson is simply this: God Almighty is in control. He sets the timeline. He establishes the agenda. He controls the calendar. Learning and accepting that, even rejoicing in it, is one of the harder lessons of faith. It is one of the most important as well. In Isaiah 5:19, the prophet pronounces a word of "woe" on the impatient: Woe to those "who say: 'Let him be quick, let him speed his work that we may see it; let the counsel of the Holy One of Israel draw near, and let it come, that we may know it!'"

God Almighty chooses to wait thirteen years at the time of life when more years cannot be taken for granted. Rather than rush in when Abram and Sarai make a misstep, he chooses to leave them to wait for his time and his agenda. If God is calling you to wait at the moment, remember times like these are an opportunity for us to learn in a fresh and deep way that God Almighty sets the timeline for his work. That is the first great lesson here about the power of God.

God establishes the identity of his covenant people

There is something very powerful about a name and something very significant about the act of naming a person or a place. When a child gets their first pet it is their privilege to give that new friend a name. Parents have a baby and it is up to them to name the child. In the days of the explorers and empire-builders, a kingdom established a new colony and gave it a name, asserting their control over that territory. The implications of that are obvious and significant. There is a great deal wrapped up in a name. In Genesis 17, our two key characters each receive a new name: a name tied to the promise of God and his covenant purposes for them:

> "When Abram was ninety-nine years old the LORD appeared to Abram and said to him, 'I am God Almighty; walk before me, and be blameless, that I may make my covenant between me and you, and may multiply you greatly.' Then Abram fell on his face. And God said to him, 'Behold, my covenant is with you, and you shall be the father of a multitude of nations. No longer shall your name be called Abram, but your name shall be Abraham, for I have made you the father of a multitude of nations. I will make you exceedingly fruitful, and I will make you into nations, and kings shall come from you'" (verses 1–6).

The name Abram meant "exalted father" but the new name the Lord gives him means "father of a multitude." God's covenant promise will now define Abraham's identity. It will require an act of faith for Abraham to bear that name before others. When he reintroduces himself to his household, family, friends, and business associates and declares that his name is now "father of a multitude," there could be occasion for a bit of scoffing or a silent chuckle.[2] After all, this 99-year-old has one child only, and that by a servant.

This new name is a declaration of divine intent, and owning that name is a declaration of faith on the part of Abraham. But more than all that, the renaming of Abram is a sign that God is claiming his life. He is reshaping and redirecting it. Abraham's very identity comes from the covenant promises and saving action of God. This is why God renames Sarai as well:

> "And God said to Abraham, 'As for Sarai your wife, you shall not call her name Sarai, but Sarah shall be her name. I will bless her, and moreover, I will give you a son by her. I will bless her, and she shall become nations; kings of peoples shall come from her'" (verses 15–16).

As far as we can tell, both "Sarai" and "Sarah" mean "princess." There is not a discernible change in meaning here, but there is a change in identity. God is claiming her life and pronouncing divine authority over her. He is insisting that her identity is shaped by his covenant promise and he is reaffirming that she is indeed a princess in the kingdom and family of God. Kings shall come from her, despite the obstacle of her barrenness.

When we come to know God through Jesus Christ, we become new people and part of a new creation. That is why Jesus renamed his disciples from time to time. We remember Simon who became Peter, a name meaning "rock," pointing to the covenant promises and purposes of God: "And I tell you, you are Peter, and on this rock I will build my church, and the gates of hell shall not prevail against it" (Matthew 16:18). When you and I come to Jesus, we receive a new identity and a new name: we once were enemies of God, but now he calls us his "friends." We once were spiritual orphans, but now we are "children of God." We once were straying and lost, but now we are the "sheep" belonging to the Great Shepherd. We once were faithless, we are now called "believers," "disciples," and "Christians." We are the very "people of God." We belong to him and we trust in his promises. Our identity and our very being are defined by knowing him and being known by him. God is in the business of renaming people because he is in the business of remaking people. He gives entirely new identities to those whom he calls and saves.

It is wonderful that the Lord does this for Abram and Sarai at this point. Chapter 16 was a low point in their rollercoaster story. Their folly in taking matters into their own hands left things in a mess. God could have given up on them and called it a day. Instead he renewed his commitment to them, gave them new names, called them his own people and set his great plans before them. There is something so hope-filled and joyful about all this. I wonder if it resonates with your own heart and touches a longing of your own soul? God makes a habit of giving people a fresh start. He takes broken, sinful, flawed, failing people with messy stories and he makes them new. Maybe your story is messy and your track record is rocky. Perhaps your burden of guilt is heavy. I hope the opportunity of a fresh start and a new identity thrills your heart.

We have all read about people who need to be given a new identity and move to a new place with a fresh start. They may be in a witness protection program. In a profound way, they start life again at that point with a new name, new story, new contacts, new identity. As those who come to the Lord for new life, we do not hide from our old contacts. The name on our passport does not change. But God does delight in making us new. For some of us, that opportunity is just what we are longing for. And the wonderful truth is that the invitation is on the table—the invitation to come to God through Jesus Christ to be made new, cleansed of sin, restored, and called God's own child. For us who have responded to this invitation, we need to make sure that we are known in the world by our new identity and called by our new name. It must have been awkward for Abram to be known by the name that signaled a promise when the promise seemed far off. It is a matter of faith for us to be known as Christians in a world that covers that name with scorn. I heard recently of a major public agency that is reportedly seeking *not* to hire Christians at the present time. That is no real surprise. We can expect more of that in the days ahead. But we have a new name, a wonderful name. It is a sign of the grace of God, a seal of his blessings and a promise of good things to come.

God establishes the requirements of covenant obedience

We all love the idea of situations where we receive benefit but have little or no obligation. The club that gives perks but makes no demands of the members; the relationship that fulfills our need for companionship but requires little of us in return; the citizenship that offers home and security but asks nothing of the people; the easy job that provides a paycheck but demands nothing beyond 9 to 5 attendance. We love to receive, but we are reluctant to be placed under obligation. Most of us are more naturally consumers than servants. This is true in many spheres of life, but especially in the matter of religion. As potential consumers of religion look at the offers on display, most would be horrified at the thought that a deity would make requirements of them if they joined. When we hear the message of grace and learn that God justifies sinners on the basis of faith, we might imagine that free salvation provides exactly what we are looking for: *a religion with free benefits and no obligation.*

At first glance, it might look like obligation-free salvation was on offer when God made those great promises to Abram "'Look toward heaven, and number the stars, if you are able to number them… So shall your offspring be.' And [Abram] believed the LORD, and he counted it to him as righteousness" (15:5–6). Abram believed that promise, and God counted that faith as righteousness. He was declared to be a righteous man, with no fear of judgment or punishment. Abram goes on to do some silly things—some sinful things—and yet he evidently remains in good standing with God. We might reflect that maybe God does not place any real demands on Abram. Maybe this is the dream situation: all benefit and no obligation. The consumer within us is stirred to delight. But if we had any misguided notions of that kind, then Genesis 17 corrects them sharply. The man whom God justified through faith is going to be called upon to walk with God in faithful obedience. Notice again how the chapter opens: God appears to Abram and says, "I am God Almighty, walk before me, and be blameless." That is what God calls his servant to do. The response of obedience is going to take a particular form for Abraham. There will be a practical and symbolic expression of this for him and his family:

> "And God said to Abraham, 'As for you, you shall keep my covenant, you and your offspring after you throughout their generations. This is my covenant, which you shall keep, between me and you and your offspring after you: Every male among you shall be circumcised'" (verses 9–10).

Every male in the household, born or bought, will be circumcised as a sign of the covenant. Anyone not circumcised will be cut off from the family (verse 14). After the debacle of chapter 16 and more than a decade of letting the dust settle, the Lord comes to Abraham and tells him in no uncertain terms that he is claiming his life and making concrete demands of him. Abram was already saved, if you like, back in Genesis 15. Circumcision is not about earning his righteousness. Salvation was a gift, freely given by God. But this is now what it will look like for Abraham to live as a saved person, set apart for the Lord.

The demand that God places upon him is personal, painful, and permanent. Abram got into trouble in the sexual realm in chapter 16, and God is now placing a mark upon his body which will speak of holiness in the sexual realm. That mark of holiness will be required not only of him, but of his children and his family. God places his claim on all of them. The covenant of circumcision is the start of God's legal requirements for his people. More will come with the Ten Commandments and the Torah, but this is the symbolic beginning. The requirement says very clearly that the God who freely justifies is the God who demands the very lives of his people. He claims all that we are and have. His saved people are his possession and are called to live his way.

In our consumer mindset, we imagine that God gives and will not take. We come and sit in a comfortable church building and meet for an hour or two with perfectly pleasant people. We step outside after the Sunday service and we imagine that our lives are ours to live as we please for the rest of the week. As Western consumers, that idea holds a great deal of appeal. We like our Christianity to be like that. But Genesis 17 tells us that the caricatured God of the Western consumer is not the God of the Bible. He claims his saved people as his very own and calls us to costly, permanent, and sometimes painful obedience to him. That is what Abraham learned that day, and that is the lesson of God's Word for us today.

We must be careful to understand that we do *not* live under the covenant of circumcision. We share in the promise that Abraham received, we are justified by faith as he was in Genesis 15. The symbolism of circumcision is fulfilled in the work of Christ and then set aside in practical terms for the Christian (see Colossians 2:11–14). The specific requirements of Genesis 17 do not apply to us today. At the same time, we need to be clear that the God of Genesis 17 has not changed. He still calls his people to be set apart, obedient, holy, and devoted to him.

The God who called Abraham to be circumcised in chapter 17 calls his people to be baptized today. Have you taken that step of obedience, being publicly set apart for him? He is the God who in Christ calls us to deny ourselves, take up our cross and follow him. He is the One who, in the Sermon on the Mount, called us, in very practical terms, to a life of holiness, honesty, sexual purity, forgiveness and grace to our enemies, and so much more besides. The God who freely gives us all things teaches us that our money is not our own. He calls us to generosity to his people and his work. The God who saves our souls is the God who claims our lives. The God who shows grace is the God who demands obedience. Where are we in danger of falling short of his calling today?

For all his failings and weaknesses, Abraham has so much to teach us about the life of faith. When the Lord spoke to him, notice how Abraham responded:

> "When he had finished talking with him, God went up from Abraham. Then Abraham took Ishmael his son and all those born in his house or bought with his money, every male among the men of Abraham's house, and he circumcised the flesh of their foreskins *that very day, as God had said to him… That very day* Abraham and his son Ishmael were circumcised" (verses 22–23, 26, my emphasis).

Abraham showed no hesitation or delay in obeying the Word of God. Where is God by his Word calling you to faithful obedience? Where is he placing a claim upon your life? Is there a delay in your heart's response? Perhaps it is in some area of known sin, in your use of time or money, your handling of relationships, or the ways in which you might be serving him. Let us not be those who delay in obeying the Word of the God who saved us in his grace and who daily leads us in his love.

7

The friend of the righteous

Genesis 18

Whenever a new relationship is established—whether it is a friendship, romance, business partnership, or membership of a team—it takes a while to see how the dynamics will play out. What will this friendship be like? How will they respond to my weaknesses and failures? How will they react to my fears and concerns?

Abraham entered into a very special relationship with God back in Genesis 12. God tapped him on the shoulder, called him away from his homeland and made a series of stunning promises to him. Then God reaffirmed his promise. Abraham took God at his word and the Lord counted Abraham's faith to him as "righteousness." He was justified before God and placed in right standing before the great Judge of all. He entered into a covenant relationship with God, a relationship of settled commitment and an unbreakable bond that was marked by the sign of circumcision. We may wonder what this covenant relationship will look like, as time goes by. What will it be like for Abraham to live in this kind of relationship with the God of heaven? What kind of time and attention will this great God give to his servant? How will God respond to

Abraham's weaknesses and failings? How will he respond to his requests and his pleas? In Genesis 18 we begin to see some of the relational dynamics play out. For those of us who have been made righteous through faith in Jesus, Genesis 18 contains deep insight into what it looks like to live in vital relationship with the God of heaven. It shows how the Lord relates to the righteous and how the righteous are to relate to him.

The Lord pursues fellowship with the righteous

There is something very special about going to someone's home and sitting down for a meal together. We have a family photograph from the 1930s which records the day when King George VI and Queen Elizabeth the Queen Mother came to visit my wife's great-grandparents at their home for tea! It is a striking picture, commemorating a rather remarkable event. But that incident, memorable as it may be, pales into insignificance compared with what happens in this chapter. The centerpiece of Genesis 18 is a home visit paid by God to his servant Abraham, accompanied by two angels. It is surely the most incredible home visit ever made.

Picture the scene: Abraham is sitting by the door of his tent in the heat of the day. He is cooling himself in the shade, perhaps after a busy morning checking over his business operations, and maybe chatting with members of his extended household who walk by. It is probably a day like any other day. But while Abraham sits at the door of his tent, lo and behold, the Lord himself appears to him. We are told that there are three men who come (verse 2). One of them is the Lord (verse 1), and we gather later that two of them are angels (19:1). Abraham seems to recognize that. He runs from the tent door and bows himself to the ground, calling his visitor "Lord" (verses 2–3). Remember, Abraham is 100 years old and a man of stature in the region. He does not run and bow to the ground before everyone who passes his tent. But he sees that he has very special visitors and so his hospitality goes beyond even the politest Middle Eastern customs. He entreats them to come in and have a meal. They agree, so he rushes to Sarah and asks her to get baking. Then he runs out to the herd and finds a calf to slaughter. The food is prepared and Abraham respectfully sets it before them, remaining standing and ready to serve, while these very special guests sit and eat. In these brief moments, Abraham and his family gain the remarkable distinction of having had the Lord and his angels to a feast in their home. It is certainly a story to tell the grandchildren.

Human beings were made for relationship with God. From the opening scenes of Genesis, we learn we were made to enjoy fellowship with our Maker. In the Garden of Eden, God came down to walk and talk with Adam in the cool of the day. There was something wonderfully wholesome and right about the first human being enjoying that time of relationship with the God who created him. But with Adam and Eve's rebellion, that time of innocence and joy ended abruptly when they were sent away from his presence. Yet God did not give up on the idea of friendship and fellowship with his created people. In fact, in calling Abram, declaring him righteous, and entering into covenant with him, God was taking steps to restore what was lost in the Fall. The image of the Lord dining at Abraham's table is a picture of restored relationship, of barriers broken down, of fellowship and even friendship.

In James 2:23 we read that Abraham was called "a friend of God." The idea that the living God would make a flawed and fallen man, a mere creature, his *friend* is remarkable. That he would come as a traveler to his tent and linger there for a meal is extraordinary. Throughout the Bible we see that God's heart is for his people. We see it when the Son of God becomes human, enters our world, and lives among us that we might know him. We see it when Jesus sits for a meal with his disciples in the Upper Room and calls us to join in that meal at the Lord's Supper. We see it in Revelation 3:20 when the Lord says to a spiritually lukewarm people, "Behold, I stand at the door and knock. If anyone hears my voice and opens the door, I will come in to him and eat with him, and he with me." We see it in Revelation 19:9 when we hear about the marriage supper of the Lamb, to which the redeemed people of God are invited for a day to come.

The idea that a sinful person could be a friend of God comes into full flower in the New Testament, and it is the idea at the heart of the gospel. In John 15, Jesus tells us that he has called his disciples his "friends." Amazing as it may seem, the Lord wants friendship with each one of us. It may be that no one goes out of their way to be your friend, and this is a particular source of sadness in your life. But consider this: the God of heaven desires friendship with you and has gone to very great lengths to make you his friend. He has traveled, as it were,through the heat of the day to be with us. In the person of his Son, he has entered our world, suffered scorn and abuse, died the death that we deserve, and borne our sin at the cross. That is the journey he took to reach us and win us as his friends. He wants to welcome us into his presence and feast with us. The story of the Bible leads to a wedding banquet when the Lord Jesus and his bride, the church, come together in a day of great celebration. Genesis 18 provides a picture of that desire and intention as the Lord approaches the home of his servant.

In Abraham, we see a model to follow. Abraham ran to meet his God, called him "Lord," bowed to the earth, and gave the very best of his household store to welcome him. He honored the Lord and welcomed him in with joy, enthusiasm, and humility. It is a simple but important lesson for us. It may be that some of us are like the lukewarm believers of Laodicea in Revelation 3.

We find that the Lord is now standing at the doorway rather than sitting at the table. He has not left us, of course, but he is now standing outside, knocking. He wants us to repent of whatever has kept him at a distance, open the door, welcome him in, and renew that friendship and closeness. Listen again to the Lord's invitation:

> "Those whom I love, I reprove and discipline, so be zealous and repent. Behold, I stand at the door and knock. If anyone hears my voice and opens the door, I will come in to him and eat with him and he with me" (Revelation 3:19–20).

As you think about how God wants to sit with us and enjoy fellowship together, it may awaken something in your heart and rouse a memory of what it was like knowing the Lord and walking with him in days gone by. Days of warm fellowship with him, enjoying time with him in his Word, and talking with him in prayer. Maybe these are *wistful* thoughts because you know that things have grown cold of late and that you have been holding him at a distance. Would you, like Abraham, welcome him afresh with honor and joy, with all that you have to give him, all the best of your life to set before him? The Lord wants fellowship with the righteous.

The Lord is patient with the righteous

Often the real test of a relationship comes when there is some kind of setback or disappointment. Most relationships work fine when there are no pressure points. But what about when things are complicated? How will the relationship go when I let my friend down? When I fail or disappoint?

At this point in the story, we turn to Abraham's wife, Sarah. The three men ask Abraham where Sarah is. It turns out that she is nearby, out of sight but listening at the tent door. The Lord says to Abraham, "I will surely return to you about this time next year, and Sarah your wife shall have a son" (verse 10). In response the 90-year-old Sarah laughs to herself. God is at the family table speaking his great promise and reaffirming what he has said before, and Sarah's response is to laugh at his word. This is obviously not the ideal response of faith—although from a human perspective, we can perhaps understand it. The whole notion of a baby sounds absurd, but for the fact that God said it. The Lord is not angry or upset, but nor does he just brush it off:

> "The LORD said to Abraham, 'Why did Sarah laugh and say, "Shall I indeed bear a child, now that I am old?" Is anything too hard for the LORD? At the appointed time I will return to you, about this time next year, and Sarah shall have a son'" (verses 13–14).

The Lord does not get angry, and he does not change his mind. He does not threaten to take his blessing elsewhere. He reaffirms his promise. Despite this graciousness, out of fear and probably some embarrassment, Sarah digs herself in deeper: "But Sarah denied it, saying, 'I did not laugh,' for she was afraid" (verse 15). She adds dishonesty on top of impertinence. Perhaps now is the moment when the Lord's temper will flare and his patience run thin?

But extraordinarily, his promises and purposes for Sarah remain unchanged, despite everything. She will have Isaac and she will receive the promises of God. God is the most gracious friend, the most patient, the most forgiving friend. His friends fail him again and again, to the point that their failure becomes embarrassing, even shocking. Yet when they do, he does not lose his cool, storm out, slam the door, never to come back again. That is not what he is like.

One of the massive takeaways of Abraham and Sarah's story is the sheer patience of God with his people. We might imagine that Genesis is all about Abraham and Sarah as great heroes of faith, but that is not the case. It is about the God of grace who bears with a stumbling and slow-to-learn people. That is perhaps the biggest encouragement of all. God takes extraordinary steps to reach and to save an unworthy people and then goes to extraordinary lengths to keep them. He shows patience upon patience upon patience with his friends. We need the patience of God in our stumbling and sin and unbelief. If God had a short fuse and a quick temper, we would be without hope. But he is patient with the people he makes righteous. If you have had occasion to fear that you have exhausted the patience of God, dwell on that rich truth and deep encouragement. Maybe you feel you have let him down one too many times, you have stumbled in sin or drifted into disbelief once too often. Maybe you wonder whether God will lose his temper and storm out. That is not the God we encounter in Genesis 18. He is a patient friend. How good that is to know and remember.

The Lord hears the intercessions of the righteous

One of the best things about friendship is opening up about your thoughts and plans, listening to their concerns, reactions and ideas, and chewing things over together. In this passage, to our great surprise, we see God do that very thing with Abraham. The heavenly visitors are leaving Abraham's tent. In verse 16, they set off toward the city of Sodom, and Abraham accompanies them as they depart. The Lord knows what is coming next and asks: "Shall I hide from Abraham what I am about to do?" (verse 17). Abraham understands what the Lord is planning to do. "Abraham drew near and said, 'Will you indeed sweep away the righteous with the wicked?'" (verses 22–23).

At this point we enter one of the most dramatic and frankly surprising interactions ever recorded between God and one of his people. Abraham has the boldness to engage in something that almost looks like haggling with the God of the Universe, the Judge of all the earth. Abraham has a boldness here that most of us would not have with our boss at work, let alone the God of heaven. If an employee began haggling and negotiating like this, you might expect their boss to lose patience and tire of their services rather quickly. If a child did this at home, he or she might find out that their parent's fuse was rather short. But Abraham presses on and, to our astonishment, God allows it. We need to understand the specific dynamics of what Abraham is doing. Remember he is a righteous man, known by God and in good standing with him on the basis of faith, not works. Abraham knows that judgment is about to fall on a wicked city. He is not asking God to ignore the wicked and their sin, but he wants to make sure that any righteous people within the city will not be swept away in judgment. He is probably particularly concerned about his nephew Lot and his household now living in Sodom.

Abraham is a righteous man interceding for the righteous. Abraham begins: "Suppose there are fifty righteous within the city. Will you then sweep away the place and not spare it for the fifty righteous who are in it?" (verse 24). Having made his opening plea, Abraham now appeals to the character of God in words that are justly famous:

> "Far be it from you to do such a thing, to put the righteous to death with the wicked, so that the righteous fare as the wicked! Far be that from you! Shall not the Judge of all the earth do what is just?" (verse 25).

Lord, I know judgment is coming on Sodom. I know they deserve it. But what if there are 50 of your righteous people within the city? Will you not hold back your judgment for their sake? Far be it from you to execute your judgment on those who ought not to be judged. Shall not you, the just Judge, do what is just?

Of course, God will do what is just. He always does. He always will. In gracious condescension and in perfect justice and fairness, the Lord answers Abraham, "If I find in Sodom fifty righteous in the city, I will spare the whole place for their sake" (verse 26). For the rest of the passage, Abraham pursues the issue: What about 45? What about 40? What about 30? What about 20? What about 10? Each time, the Lord confirms that for such a number of righteous, he will spare the city.

As with everything else recorded in Scripture, it is good to stand back from the drama and ask why the Lord caused this both to happen and to be recorded here. After all, the Lord could have shut down this conversation before it began or left no record of it, but it is here for us in the pages of Scripture for a reason. In his work of judgment and salvation, God is totally fair and just. In his work of bringing judgment to the wicked, he is patient and careful. The care of God in all this is remarkable: "I will go down to see whether they have done altogether according to the outcry that has come to me. And if not, I will know" (verse 21).

No doubt there are far too many people in prison in this world who have languished for years for crimes they did not commit. We rightly ask whether the judge paid proper attention to the facts. Did he read the case file thoroughly? Did she take account of all the evidence? A sloppy judge is a fearful thing. There are plenty of heartbreaking stories of wrongful conviction—but never with the Lord. Abraham declares that the Judge of all the earth will do what is just, and that is exactly what we see in action here. God is just and fair. What a comfort that is. We see something else as well. We see that God listens. His righteous servant comes to him and pleads for the righteous. Wonderfully, strikingly, reassuringly, the just Judge hears. In this exchange with Abraham, we are witnessing something that is repeated and amplified as the story of salvation progresses. As this righteous man intercedes for the righteous, we see a gospel pattern that will flower fully when the Lord Jesus comes and dies for sin and rises again, ascending to heaven as our Great High Priest.

The Bible tells us that the Greater Son of Abraham, the truly righteous Man, is even now at the right hand of the Father, interceding for his righteous people. The book of Hebrews tells us that Jesus our Great High Priest lives to make intercession for us (Hebrews 7:25). 1 John 2:1 gives us the reassurance that "we have an advocate with the Father, Jesus Christ the righteous." We may ask why it matters that we have a righteous advocate before God the Judge and why it matters for us to know that God will listen to intercessions on behalf of his people. It matters because we are a flawed and failing people. We are a people who sin and let our Lord down, again and again. Added to that, we live in a world headed for divine judgment. There may be times when we wonder if we are in fact headed for the flood of destruction along with the wicked. The reassurance we have here is that there is One in the throne room of heaven, whose work it is to advocate for us before the Father. This righteous One calls upon the Judge of all the earth to do what is just, and not to sweep away with the wicked those whom he has made righteous by his blood.

The story of Abraham in Genesis 18 gives us a window into what will be happening in heaven even now. The Judge of all the earth is just and he will listen to the Righteous One and do what is right for the sake of his righteous people. What is it like to be a friend of God? It is a privileged position. It is enjoying friendship with the God who wants to know you and have fellowship with you. It is sitting down at the banqueting table with him. It is being a recipient of his patience. How we need his patience! It is sheltering under his justice and mercy, even as our advocate pleads our case before the throne. There is no greater privilege than to live in covenant relationship and vital friendship with the God of heaven. Do you know that friendship? Are you enjoying it today?

8

The judgment and mercy of God

Genesis 19

It has often been noted that we are a generation with muddled priorities. We easily confuse the relative importance of worship, work and play. It has been quipped that we work at our play, worship our work, and play at our worship.[1] Too often even real believers who know and love Jesus Christ treat lightly the things of God. Genesis 19 is one of the most unsettling chapters in the Bible. It is an account of terrible wickedness and fearful judgment, and it is meant to wake us up. If we merely play at our worship, Genesis 19 should cause us to take seriously the things of God and to feel the weightiness of eternal matters. The city of Sodom has been under a fearful cloud throughout much of Abraham's story: "the men of Sodom were wicked, great sinners against the LORD" (13:13). The Lord and two angels left Abraham, and continued on their way to Sodom. There was a foreboding surrounding their visit. "Because the outcry against Sodom and Gomorrah is great and their sin is very grave, I [the Lord] will go down to see whether they have done altogether according to the outcry that has come to me" (18:20–21).

Lot is part of God's chosen family, but through his own ill-advised choices, he finds himself living in the midst of a wicked city bound for destruction. The events that now transpire and the judgment that falls upon Sodom are harrowing.

We are to take seriously the judgment of God

You may have seen the photograph of the atomic bomb that was dropped on the city of Hiroshima on August 6th, 1945. It is extraordinary to think of destruction coming upon a city so suddenly and decisively. The people were going about their business—eating in cafes, shopping in the supermarket, meeting in the local park. Suddenly, it was all brought to a dramatic end.

Just recently archeologists working in the ancient city of Pompeii released poignant photographs of the outlines of two bodies discovered in a villa just outside the city. The eruption of Mount Vesuvius in October AD 79 left the fossilized city remarkably preserved under a great cloud of ash and the two bodies were found lying in the house, precisely where they fell when disaster struck. It is fearful to think of people going about their daily lives and suddenly being overtaken by calamity. Pompeii stands as a monument to the sheer fragility of human life and human civilization.

The Bible tells us we live in a world under judgment. On a day yet to be revealed, the judgment of God will be released on the place where we live and the world we inhabit. Unlike the people of Hiroshima or Pompeii, we have been warned and know it is coming. For now, life continues as normal. We go about our business and live our lives, even as they did. When the sun is out and life is pleasant and the community is buzzing, it is difficult to take seriously the idea that God will judge the world as he says he will.

The first and greatest lesson from the destruction of Sodom is that God notices sin in his world, and he is committed to dealing with it. Back in Genesis 18 we saw that God knew what was going on in Sodom and was committed to investigating it. The outcry had reached his ears (18:20) and he would go and see for himself. When the two angels go to Sodom, the men of the city hear of the newcomers and want to assault them. Lot offers the men hospitality, aware that if they stay in the town square they will be in danger. Lot knows what the people of Sodom are like. The account of what happens next is harrowing. The men of the city call out to Lot, "Where are the men who came to you tonight? Bring them out to us, that we may know them" (verse 5). When Lot refuses to bow to the pressure, they respond: "'Stand back!... This fellow came to sojourn, and he has become the judge! Now we will deal worse with you than with them.' Then they pressed hard against the man Lot and drew near to break the door down" (verse 9).

This was a city marked by violence and sexual immorality. That is clear enough from the account and is confirmed by the New Testament. The language that Jude 7 uses is this: "Sodom and Gomorrah and the surrounding cities... indulged in sexual immorality and pursued unnatural desire." We know how events soon unfold. A very dramatic judgment of God falls upon the city. Just try and picture it in your mind's eye. Lot has fled with his immediate family and now comes the promised judgment of God:

> "Then the LORD rained down on Sodom and Gomorrah sulfur and fire from the LORD out of heaven. And he overthrew those cities, and all the valley, and all the inhabitants of the cities, and what grew on the ground" (verses 24–25).

Abraham was looking on from a distance. As he looked, "the smoke of the land went up like the smoke of a furnace" (verse 28). Sulfur and fire fall from heaven. That is what God does here in response to sin. That outpouring of judgment is, according to the Bible, a pale foretaste of what is to come. In 2 Peter 2:6, we are told explicitly that the destruction of Sodom is a foretaste and a warning of the coming judgment, "an example of what is going to happen to the ungodly." Peter goes on:

> "… the day of the Lord will come like a thief, and then the heavens will pass away with a roar, and the heavenly bodies will be burned up and dissolved, and the earth and the works that are done on it will be exposed… the heavens will be set on fire and dissolved, and the heavenly bodies will melt as they burn" (2 Peter 3:10, 12).

That is the future. That is what is coming.

We have to stand back and process the simple and startling point: God notices sin in a wicked society. He does not tolerate sin in his world. He will bring his judgment upon his creation in a day to come. Our society has been so hard at work normalizing all kinds of sin, not least, sexual sin. Perhaps the last great social evil in our society is the evil of criticizing or questioning someone else's behavior, especially in this realm. We know that the Bible clearly teaches that marriage between a man and a woman is the only right context for sexual intimacy. Yet that clearly was not the accepted norm in Sodom, and it is by no means the accepted norm in our society today. As believers, we have to constantly re-set our ethical framework to conform it to the Word of God. We need to do so personally because each of us easily strays from God's Word. We are far from perfect, far from blameless in this. We need deep humility and constant repentance when we think about ethics, sin and judgment. The church of Jesus Christ can hardly claim a record of flawlessness when it comes to any type of sin, sexual sin being no exception. We need to be reminded that God's Word is unchanging and his judgments unfailing.

Within the story of Sodom's destruction, some of the greatest tragedies are seen in the lives of those who simply will not take the warning seriously. When the angels warned Lot to flee, they asked if he had loved ones in the city—sons-in-law, daughters and so on. Lot rushed to his sons-in-law: "Up! Get out of this place for the LORD is about to destroy the city." But then we read the tragic words: "But he seemed to his sons-in-law to be jesting" (verse 14). They thought it was a ridiculous joke and they went back to clearing their emails, doing their online banking, and catching up on social media. They ignored it. On the way out of Sodom, the angels told Lot: "Escape for your life. Do not look back or stop anywhere in the valley. Escape to the hills, lest you be swept away" (verse 17). But Lot's wife looked back as they fled and became a pillar of salt (verse 26). Tragically, she failed to take seriously the warning given her.

As well as examining our own lives in a sober way, we who know the Lord also need to be prepared to speak about the truth of God's Word in our society today, graciously, lovingly, and urgently. Not that we force the morality of Scripture on others—that is not our job. But it is our responsibility and calling to warn those around us of the judgment to come and to invite and plead with them to find refuge in Christ, the one who welcomes with open arms *anyone and everyone* who will repent and believe. Lot dared to challenge the behavior of the crowd. He pleaded with them not to act wickedly, and they turned on him: "This fellow came to sojourn, and he has become the judge! Now we will deal worse with you than with them" (verse 9). Lot was terribly compromised himself, but when he dared get in the way of the crowd, they practically tore him to pieces. Today, Christians are becoming very afraid of doing or saying anything that will offend the surrounding culture. We just do not want to be attacked. We do not want to fall foul of the mores of political correctness or get into awkwardness or trouble. We are tempted simply to be quiet.

The story of Sodom reminds us that God will judge sin. No amount of social awkwardness will overturn that fact. We need to be those who will stand on the Word of God and lovingly warn our friends and neighbors of the judgment to come so that they might find salvation in Christ, as we have found it. We need to be those who grieve the sheer lostness of our society, who tremble at the fate of the unrepentant, who pray for the Lord to be gracious and to save many. This cautionary tale teaches us to take seriously the judgment of God.

We are to take seriously the mercy of God

Anyone who has had a near-death experience would likely say that the experience changed their outlook on life. They may reassess priorities, perhaps setting aside certain pursuits or abandoning certain patterns of unhealthy or ungodly behavior.

When I was growing up, I knew a man who narrowly missed traveling on the Titanic. He was due to be on the ship on its fateful maiden crossing, but he was unwell, and the family could not sail. He lived his whole life in the shadow of that disaster, knowing that he had only barely escaped. We can only imagine the impact that such an example might have, knowing your whole life that you have been spared. Lot and his family had a near-death experience in Sodom. They only escaped because of the mercy of God. The story highlights the mercy of God in a very dramatic way, particularly on the morning of the fateful day:

> "As morning dawned, the angels urged Lot, saying, 'Up! Take your wife and your two daughters who are here, lest you be swept away in the punishment of the city.' But he lingered. So the men seized him and his wife and his two daughters by the hand, the Lord being merciful to him, and they brought him out and set him outside the city" (verses 15–16).

The rescue was accomplished by divine agency and through the sheer mercy of God. It is a picture of the rescue that God has achieved for all his saved people. God rescued Lot because he remembered the covenant promises he had made to Abraham. The text is very clear: "So it was that, when God destroyed the cities of the valley, God remembered Abraham and sent Lot out of the midst of the overthrow when he overthrew the cities in which Lot had lived" (verse 29). Like Lot, we who know and trust Jesus also rely on God's covenant promises. We believe that God will spare us in the judgment to come because of the promises he has made, promises going back to Abraham. Because God is faithful, we trust he will show mercy to his family of faith, to those who believe, just as Abraham believed.

God delights in showing mercy. But we need to take that mercy seriously. When Lot received the warning, he lingered in the stricken city and practically had to be dragged out. His wife, who also received the mercy of God, clearly did not realize the full value of what she had been given. Her instruction was not to look back, but she did not take it seriously. She did not really see the true value of her rescue. She looked back and perished. This turn of events is shocking enough, but then we come to Lot's daughters. The judgment of God had fallen upon their home city. You might have thought that they would have been chastened by the experience; the smell of the sulfur from the burning city must have been etched in their memories. However, Genesis 19 ends with one of the ugliest incidents of sexual sin found in the Bible as Lot's daughters degrade themselves in a profound way. Their near-death experience clearly did not reshape their lives, nor did their experience of rescue and the mercy of God.

I find myself asking whether my experience of mercy shapes my life as it should. Do we daily live as a people who have narrowly escaped destruction? Have our values and priorities been transformed as a result? Do we have a real abhorrence of sin because we have been rescued from its penalty? Do we have a light hold on the world because we have been spared its destruction? Or do we continue to live in the same way that the citizens of this stricken city live? Have we taken seriously the mercy of God and his great rescue? Has it transformed us? We must take seriously the mercy of God.

We are to take seriously the cost of compromise

I lived for a time in Cambridge, England and enjoyed watching the punting boats on the River Cam. These "punts" are long, low boats propelled with a long stick that you drive into the riverbed and use to push the boat along as you glide through the ancient town. Down at the river on a summer's day, you might see a hapless tourist who has ended up with one foot on the boat and one on the bank, and the boat drifting quickly away! At some point the situation has to resolve itself: either both feet step onto the bank or into the boat, or else the tourist ends up doing the splits and landing in the water. Living with a foot in different places for too long is always going to end badly.[2]

The believer can find himself or herself in a similar position, trying to live long-term with one foot in the kingdom of this world and one foot in the kingdom of God. But, of course, it is not sustainable. It is dangerous and likely to end in disaster. Yet many of us try to live that precarious existence for as long as we possibly can, even though it is fundamentally compromised. Lot is the great Bible warning of a believer who lived what was clearly a compromised life. He had one foot firmly in the world and he bore the consequences of it in the end.

The roots of compromise for Lot go back to Genesis 13 when Abraham gave Lot the choice of territory, and Lot made his decision based on the physical attractiveness of the land rather than the promises of God. He went to the very edge of the Promised Land of Canaan, settling "among the cities of the valley and mov[ing] his tent as far as Sodom" (13:12).

By the next chapter, Sodom came under attack and Lot needed rescuing by Abraham. We learn that Lot was now "dwelling in Sodom" (14:12). He had settled in and ended up putting himself and his family at terrible risk from those invading kings. At the start of chapter 19, we find Lot sitting in the gate of Sodom, where the men of influence sat to discuss the affairs of the city. He has made himself at home in Sodom, and he has come to be a leading citizen. We are meant to see a contrast once again with Abraham. In chapter 18, when the Lord and two angels paid Abraham a visit, they found him by the oaks of Mamre, sitting at the door of his tent. Abraham is in the Promised Land, at his home. He is where the Lord has placed him and called him to be. But when the same angels come to Lot, he is in the gate of the wicked city in the place of networking and influence. It is a stark contrast, and we cannot fail to notice it.

Abraham is in the place of faithfulness, but Lot is in a place of compromise, and ultimately, of disaster. As Sodom burns, Abraham is watching from afar, from a place of safety, from the place where he had met with the Lord and spoken with him:

> "And Abraham went early in the morning to the place where he had stood before the LORD. And he looked down to toward Sodom and Gomorrah and toward all the land of the valley, and he looked and, behold, the smoke of the land went up like the smoke of a furnace" (verses 27–28).

It is quite a contrast. Lot is not completely like the men of Sodom—he does stand apart from them in some ways. He offers warm hospitality to the angels who come to him and invites them to eat and sleep in his home. It is good that he did, as the visitors were in danger from Sodom's citizens. Lot must have known what the people of the town were like and must have been aware of what would happen: "But before they lay down, the men of the city, the men of Sodom, both young and old, all the people to the last man, surrounded the house" (verse 4). They wanted to assault these guests and they demanded the visitors be handed over to them.

In Lot's response, we see stunning evidence of his compromise. He wants to protect his guests, which is good, but we see how far the rot has spread: "I beg you, my brothers, do not act so wickedly" (verse 7). Lot does not want them to do this wicked thing but in the same breath, he calls these wicked men his "brothers." His tone is far too familiar, too warm, too close. Then in verse 8 he does a horrific thing. He says to them: *Look, why not take my daughters instead? Do not assault these guests, you can have my own daughters. Do as you please.* It is a sickening offer and a dreadful failure in his duty of fatherly care. It is a sign of just how corrosive and compromising his situation in Sodom has become.

When Lot tries to warn his near and dear of the danger, it is so telling that his sons-in-law think it is all a joke (verse 14). Clearly these young men, who were joining Lot's family through marriage, did not know the Lord or fear him. There was no preserving the faith in the younger generations of Lot's family. When Lot escapes with his wife, the angels give the warning not to look back for fear of the Lord's destruction. It says something that Lot's wife so readily ignores the warning from heaven and looks back. In the Lord's mercy, Lot and his daughters escape. Having lost so much, we might hope that their new life would be marked with fresh devotion to the Lord, but our chapter ends with an incident that is truly appalling: the incestuous and degrading actions of Lot's daughters.

We have no indication that Lot abandoned the Lord or his faith in the Lord. In fact, the New Testament tells us the opposite; 2 Peter 2:7 says that Lot was a righteous man who was "greatly distressed by the sensual conduct of the wicked." Peter says that each day Lot was "tormenting his righteous soul over their lawless deeds that he saw and heard" (2 Peter 2:8). Lot was a believer, even as he lived in Sodom. He did not abandon the faith. But he made his home in Sodom. He sought to integrate in the community. He tried to find a way of living with the people of Sodom as his brothers, with the men at the gate as his associates, and he ended up in a place of compromise with a foot firmly in Sodom, even as he tried to keep the other foot in the kingdom of God. Lot was saved, to be sure, but look at the fallout. His daughters were engaged to godless men, they were almost thrown to the crowd of abusers, and his wife was destroyed in the judgment of God. Then his daughters degraded themselves and him in the most appalling manner. We are meant to recognize that if we try to pursue a home in this world, with one foot in the world and one foot in the kingdom of God, the Lord may be gracious to us and save us, but it is going to be costly. We may escape judgment, but only as those escaping through fire (1 Corinthians 3:15).

I say this with sadness, but I think it is fair to say that if we are parents, our compromise is likely to be particularly costly for our children. Far too often believing parents—perhaps of fine, believing stock of generations gone by—seek to make their home in this world. They pursue wholeheartedly worldly things and worldly status and pleasures. They make their closest associates the people of the city about them. They may hold on to their faith themselves in a somewhat half-hearted way, but their children, after observing the awkward compromise of their parents, what will they choose? I have so often seen (and perhaps you have too) the way that the children will abandon the kingdom of God and choose to jump on the shore of the kingdom of this world. They do not bother with the awkward compromise their parents sought to maintain. They will just go for the world and jump in with both feet. Compromise is costly. We need to hear the warning and we need to take it seriously.

I trust we are not those who in any sense play at our worship, who take lightly the things of God. May his judgment and his mercy not be light things to us. All who love God will want to take to heart what the Bible is saying, flee the judgment to come, and run to Jesus and his cross. Have you received the mercy of God? Are you rejoicing in his salvation? Are both your feet firmly in the kingdom, with your hope set fully on the city that is to come?

9

An unflattering comparison

Genesis 20

I often find that the surprises of Scripture hold some of the richest lessons for us. I have come to love the surprises of the Bible, because through them God reshapes my thinking and teaches me new things about himself. Genesis 20 is a chapter full of surprising truths about us and about God—truths that we need to learn and take to heart as we go forward in the Christian life.

Do not be surprised when patterns of sin repeat themselves

I wonder if you have ever had an unwelcome experience of déjà vu? Perhaps you go through a messy or disappointing or challenging situation and suddenly realize you have been here before. *I can hardly believe it. I thought I had learnt these lessons last time, but here I am again.*

We have been working on a couple of redecorating projects in our house. I know from experience how important it is to put down protective covering on surfaces such as the carpets and furniture. But covering every square inch takes a lot of time and effort, and I always want to get on with the painting. So I rush on, and the results are predictable. I find myself, yet again, on hands and knees trying desperately to scrub paint out of the carpet with that unfortunate sensation of déjà vu.

More seriously, you may experience times of difficulty or tension in a relationship and start to recognize your own wrongdoing in the situation. You work things through, you make amends, you move forward. But then in six months, or a year, or ten years, you slip into your old patterns of behavior. Tensions rise, and you are back precisely where you were, accompanied by a sinking sense of *déjà vu*.

Genesis 20 is a major case of *déjà vu* in the life of Abraham. In chapter 19, Abraham observed the judgment that fell on the wicked cities of Sodom and Gomorrah. Now Abraham and Sarah, semi-nomads that they were, are on the move again to new pastures, journeying south-west, toward the territory of the Negeb, sojourning in Gerar. As they move into this unfamiliar territory, which was evidently controlled by an unknown king, Abraham starts thinking defensively. He knows that his wife has attracted attention in other places. We can only assume that her beauty has not faded, despite her very advanced age at this point. It might stand to reason that she has an unusually youthful appearance as she will bear a child in the next chapter.

This defensive pattern of thought is not new for Abraham. He has shown this kind of cowardice before, putting his own wellbeing ahead of the sanctity of his marriage and ahead of the honor and safety of his wife. The ruse of verse 2, shocking as it is, does not come out of nowhere: "And Abraham said of Sarah his wife, 'She is my sister.' And Abimelech king of Gerar sent and took Sarah." This is a half-lie; Abraham and Sarah are half-siblings. But, more importantly, they are husband and wife. There is no doubt that Abraham's presentation is calculated to deceive. Mercifully, the Lord intervenes before Sarah joins the king's harem, averting disaster: "But God came to Abimelech in a dream by night and said to him, 'Behold, you are a dead man because of the woman whom you have taken, for she is a man's wife'" (verse 3).

The narrative is designed to ring some bells in our memories. Back in Genesis 12, right at the start of the Abraham story, about 25 years before the events of this chapter, Abraham did the very same thing in Egypt. Sarai caught the eye of Pharaoh, who took her as his wife, thinking she was Abram's unmarried sister. Sarai was dishonored and Abram's witness to the Lord was in tatters. Genesis 20 represents a remarkable repetition of disastrous behavior. In fact, the resonances of the story with chapter 12 are so striking that a number of critical scholars feel that this is just a literary cut and paste job. They say that the original story has been repeated here with names changed. I do not buy that for a moment. I think the true repetition of these events carries deep lessons for us, particularly about the human heart and the reality of sin.

In chapter 12, Abraham was just starting out on his journey. The Lord had just called him and made his great promises to him. He experienced a terrible failure and a terrible fall, but since then Abraham has matured. He has witnessed the Lord at work. He has learned something of God's faithfulness. He has seen quite a lot of his own heart and learned a few things about himself. But here he is, all these years later, having known some great spiritual victories, having been a model of faith on so many occasions, reacting in precisely the same way again when presented with the same temptation to cowardice and dishonesty. Verses 1 and 2 read so plainly and so starkly. Before they even unpack their toothbrushes or set up the campfire or find the nearest supermarket, they lie: "And Abraham said of Sarah his wife, 'She is my sister'" (verse 2). If there had been imminent danger or threat or pressure, we might have a little more sympathy. But it seems like this is an unprompted move, an unforced error. It seems such a surprise. *Surely, Abraham has grown? Surely, he has matured? Is he not beyond this kind of stupidity now?* Sadly, he is not.

It is remarkable, and we are meant to take note. What is true of our faith-hero Abraham is true of us, in very large measure. Our situation is different, of course. We live under the New Covenant and not under the Old. If we belong to Christ, we are filled with the Holy Spirit in a way that believers in the Old Testament were not. We live after the Day of Pentecost and not before. In the Old Testament, the Spirit of God came upon key servants at key times and for key purposes, but there was not a permanent indwelling of the kind that we know today. Abraham was not without the Spirit's intervention in his life, but he was not living this side of Pentecost either. There is a degree of privilege attached to our situation that Old Testament believers did not have in the same way. However, the reality of the sinful nature is not done away with by the indwelling of the Spirit of God. We have a new power, but this side of heaven, we still have to contend with our old nature within, as Abraham did. His experience as a man of faith is here to teach us and, in this case, to warn us.

If you ever go for a walk in the countryside or in the woods, sometimes you will find a trail that has been used for trucks or tractors, an unpaved track that has been traveled again and again. When you drive down an earthen track like that, your wheels naturally settle into the groove of the track. You could almost let go of the steering wheel and the grooves would direct you. Likewise, over time, sin carves ruts in our hearts.[1] There are grooves of sin formed through repeated temptation and failure that get worn into us. I want to suggest that we are a little naive if we think that those grooves will just disappear. We are setting ourselves up for rather dramatic failure if we imagine that things that tempted us or caused us to stumble five, ten, or twenty years ago, somehow will not trouble us any more. Here, Abraham is faced with precisely the same circumstance that he had faced a quarter of a century earlier, and without pausing for breath, he fell into precisely the same sin. It is as though 25 years of learning and growing and walking with the Lord had not happened.

To think you are not at all like Abraham in that puts you in a place of real spiritual vulnerability. Temptation does not disappear this side of heaven. The ruts in our heart carved by sin are not normally erased by the Spirit of God. He helps us not to slide into them, he gives us grace, he is more than able to keep us from falling. We grow in strength and maturity and godliness. But, in most cases, the ruts are still there. The vulnerabilities continue to exist, and we need to be fully aware of that as we move forward in the Christian life. It is important to underline this because we can have those seasons where we are doing well and growing and feeling the help of the Spirit. We can think to ourselves that the old, habitual, besetting sins are no longer a danger for us: *I have been healed of that. I have been set free.* And we let our guard down. Well, be careful, you who think you stand, lest you fall (1 Corinthians 10:12). When you feel a sense of victory, and complacency sets in, that is a dangerous season.

Where are the grooves carved in your heart? Maybe they are to do with your temper, or your tongue, or some kind of sexual temptation. Maybe they are to do with greed, or dishonesty, or something else altogether. You will know your heart. Let me encourage you to be on your guard. Let me warn you from the example of Abraham, as I warn myself: the grooves do not readily disappear. By the help of the Spirit, let us be remain alert because patterns of sin can so easily repeat themselves.

Do not be surprised when God is at work in unbelievers

What the Lord does here in the heart and life of Abimelech is quite incredible and not what Abraham would have expected. Abimelech takes Sarah into his house, and God comes to him in a dream and tells him he is in big trouble (verse 3). In Abimelech's response, we see something quite surprising within the heart of this king who knows nothing of the Lord:

> "Now Abimelech had not approached her. So he said, 'Lord, will you kill an innocent people? Did he not himself say to me, "She is my sister"? And she herself said, "He is my brother." In the integrity of my heart and the innocence of my hands I have done this.' Then God said to him in the dream, 'Yes, I know that you have done this in the integrity of your heart, and it was I who kept you from sinning against me. Therefore I did not let you touch her'" (verses 4–6).

This is really something. Here is a pagan king, by no means a follower of the Lord or a member of the family of faith, acting decently. He actually acts in a far better manner than Abraham. If there is one figure in the story who comes out well here, it is Abimelech. Remarkably the Lord speaks to him in this very personal way and reveals that he has been at work in his life, restraining him from doing evil.

This is, if you like, a very startling example of what theologians sometimes call "common grace." "Special grace" or "saving grace" is God's work of grace by his Spirit that is shown in the lives of those whom he saves. But God also works by *common grace* to restrain sin in the world and to enable people—unbelievers—to do things that are kind and decent and beneficial in varying measure. Genesis 20 is an amazing example of that. God has restrained evil in this man and has been at work in his life by his sovereignty. Abraham had little concept of this and no confidence of it. He tells us as much when Abimelech quite reasonably asks him why on earth he has behaved in the way that he has. Abraham's answer betrays so much: "I did it because

I thought, 'There is no fear of God at all in this place, and they will kill me because of my wife'" (verse 11). *I am going into a snake pit here,* thought Abraham, *into a territory where Gentiles rule and where there is no knowledge of God.* That may have been true enough but, in going into unbelieving territory, he was wrong to imagine that he was going into territory where God was not able to work in lives and restrain evil. God is able to do work in any life, in any culture, in any part of the world because, whether people acknowledge him or not, he is their Sovereign Creator and he holds their heart in his hand.

Frankly, there will be times when unbelievers will put us to shame by their good behavior. We have all seen that, I am sure. The traffic jam that makes you impatient and pushy, when other drivers are being gracious and waving people on. A contentious issue in the community provokes some Christian friends to post angry or discourteous messages on social media, while unbelievers in the neighborhood are careful and kind in what they say. It happens, and, while it puts us to shame, the good behavior of outsiders actually points to God's kindness. It shows his common grace at work in their lives, restraining evil and making fallen society live-able–which, of course, it would not be without the Spirit's intervention. The reputational damage here for Abraham is unavoidable. Abimelech notices and reprimands Abraham: "What have you done to us? And how have I sinned against you, that you have brought on me and my kingdom a great sin?" (verse 9). *Why have you behaved so badly, Abraham?* Frankly, Abimelech looks like the righteous one here, due to common grace. And Abraham, for one, did not expect it.

Why does it matter to us to understand that God can work in this way? Why do we need a robust theology of common grace? It tells us that we do not need to go into the world terrified of what unbelievers will do to us, quivering at the darkness.

We can easily fall into this trap, especially as we see our culture darkening and becoming less receptive to the gospel. But we must not go out into society imagining that the Lord will leave us to sink in the mire or thinking that compromise and fearful self-protection is the only way forward. That is what Abraham did. He assumed that the people around him would only do evil, that he would get hurt and that his only recourse was deception and, bluntly, to throw his wife to the wolves.

As society darkens and as culture moves further and further away from any kind of historic Christian values, the danger is that we will throw our hands up in despair and declare "There is no fear of God in this place." The danger is that we will adopt a fearful and defensive posture, like Abraham did. But that will not go well. We will make bad decisions, pragmatic and faithless ones, if we assume that God is powerless to intervene and is going to throw us to the wolves. We must remember that he is *not* powerless, and he will not abandon his people. It is incredible how the incident here with Abimelech the unbeliever ends:

> "Then Abimelech took sheep and oxen, and male servants and female servants, and gave them to Abraham, and returned Sarah his wife to him. And Abimelech said, 'Behold, my land is before you; dwell where it pleases you.' To Sarah he said, 'Behold, I have given your brother a thousand pieces of silver. It is a sign of your innocence in the eyes of all who are with you, and before everyone you are vindicated'" (verses 14–16).

This is an object lesson for Abraham and Sarah, and for us too, in God's common grace. We are not to be surprised when God is at work in unbelievers. He has power to move the heart of non-Christians to do good and decent things and he has power to work in society for the sake of his people.

Do not be surprised when God continues to use stumbling servants

We are often slow to understand and appreciate the sheer patience and forbearance of God. It is a remarkable thing that God puts up with his people. It is remarkable that he puts up with me and it is remarkable that he puts up with you. I hope you have a sense of wonder at his patience and forbearance. If we have any shred of honesty about ourselves, we have to admit that we are deeply flawed, continually sinful, and repeatedly failing servants of God. This is just the reality for redeemed sinners who are works of sanctification in progress. Yes, the Spirit is changing us, but how slow and reluctant we are to grow. Some of us will have a profound sense of this. We stumble and sin, we fail and we may fall, and we wonder repeatedly whether God has any more time for us or can use us any longer.

If you ever ponder that question, this part of Abraham's story has deep comfort and encouragement for you. If God should have given up on any servant of his, frankly, he should have given up on Abraham. We look at him here next to the pagan king, and the pagan looks like a paradigm of virtue and righteousness, while Abraham looks… well, rather less impressive. Abimelech and his crew are not believers, but they understand the fear of God on some level. Abimelech hears the voice of God, and notice how he responds: "So Abimelech rose early in the morning and called all his servants and told them all these things. And the men were very much afraid" (verse 8). Abraham, for his part, knows *fear* in this chapter but it is not primarily the fear of the Lord, it is rather the fear of a godless people. We might well ask: *Why did you do this, Abraham?* "I did it because I thought, 'There is no fear of God at all in this place, and they will kill me because of my wife'" (verse 11). *What about your fear of God Abraham? What about your trust in him? What about your call to obey him?* With his repeat offence of dishonesty, and of dishonoring his wife and his marriage vows, we wonder how God can put up with him any longer. With his terrible witness to the pagan king for a second time around, surely the depths of the patience of God are now exhausted. It is not like he is a new convert. We are a quarter of a century into the covenant relationship, and Abraham has been so very privileged... But all the way through this messy and ugly incident, God remains steadfast in his resolve to protect and even to use Abraham. Notice what the Lord says to Abimelech in verse 7—it jumps off the page—"Now then, return the man's wife, *for he is a prophet*, so that he will pray for you, and you shall live." *What? Lord, haven't you fired Abraham? Aren't you going to quietly put him on desk duty now, sideline him and move on? You're declaring him a prophet?*

This is the very first time in the Bible that anyone is called a prophet. The prophetic office is a big deal in Scripture. It is a role that points ultimately to Jesus, the supreme prophet who comes to earth to speak God's final word. Abraham has the honor of being the first person to receive that declaration and hold that office. The announcement that Abraham is a prophet comes *here*, and it comes *now*. The Lord is showing us that he does not give up easily on his people. He is showing us that he uses failed and fumbling, sinful and stumbling people to do his work. He is showing us the sheer depths of his mercy and kindness.

I do not know if you have ever had the experience of speaking with a parent about their adult son or daughter who is frankly a bit of a mess. Their offspring may have made some bad decisions and are clearly not on the right track but this parent is misty-eyed when talking about their beloved child. The parent speaks of their delight in them, how pleased they are about the good things in their lives, their gifts and abilities, and how much potential they see. You reserve comment, but can hardly help thinking: *Are we talking about the same person here? Is this parent not just a little deluded?* Maybe they are. Or maybe they are just parents who dream the best and pray the best and decide to see the best, as parents often do. There is no delusion in Genesis 20. The Lord is totally realistic about Abraham, of course. But we do see his fatherly heart. His wayward son is not about to be disinherited or thrown out of the family business because he has stumbled yet again.

The Lord follows through on what he says he will do:

> "Then Abraham prayed to God, and God healed Abimelech, and also healed his wife and female slaves so that they bore children. For the LORD had closed all the wombs of the house of Abimelech because of Sarah, Abraham's wife" (verse 17–18).

The Lord was still pleased to hear the prayers of Abraham and to work powerfully in response. It is wonderful how the Lord continues to use Abraham. The fact that he does so gives hope and encouragement to us. It says to us that our failures do not render us useless to God. It says to us that he does not reach a point of frustration, a point when he just gives up on us.

How we need to know that because, frankly, we might have given up on ourselves long ago. If you are aware of being flawed and failing, a sinful and stumbling servant, and you wonder if there is any patience left for you in the heart of God or in his plans, take comfort from the story of Abraham. God does not give up on his servants, and he does not cast them aside. Even more wonderfully, none of this in any way depends on Abraham. At least, *not ultimately*. Abraham's performance, his faithfulness and obedience, are not the source or engine of God's plans here. At the end of the day, Abraham is not the hero of this story. In fact, in this chapter, he is a kind of anti-hero who points us to the true hero of the story.

Back in chapter 15, when God spoke his covenant promises to Abraham, we were told that Abraham believed the LORD, and it was credited to him as righteousness (15:6). Abraham trusted God, and God gave to him the gift of righteousness through faith. That gift of right standing ultimately comes through the true hero who would arrive centuries later. The true Savior would come and would obey the Father perfectly, trust him fully, and he would lay down his life willingly. At the cross, Jesus paid the price for Abraham's failure and for your failure and for mine. The failure of Abraham here and the fact that he is so obviously not the hero, so obviously sinful and not worthy, demonstrates that his standing before God and his usefulness to God have *nothing* to do with himself, and everything to do with the one who would make him righteous through shedding his own blood. Genesis 20 is full of grace and full of the gospel because it shows redemption in action. It shows God using and persevering with someone who is not worthy. He does it because of the Savior who would come. Continue to delight in his grace and his patience and forbearance to you. Give yourself, in trust, to his service, with all your stumbling and sin, confident that he can use even you.

10

The God of astounding faithfulness

Genesis 21

Let me describe someone to you. This is a person you like and appreciate, maybe even love, whose company you enjoy and whose opinion you value. But this is also someone you know you cannot always rely on 100 percent. They say they are booking time for you on Thursday. They might show up, but you should probably not hold your breath. You bought a joint present for someone with them; it is on your credit card and they owe you their 50 percent, but you may as well write off that money now. There is a job they have committed to do, but you had better be ready to do it yourself. In this relationship, you always have to have a backup plan. You have to prepare for some disappointment. Most of us have experienced a relationship like that at some point and have developed some coping mechanisms. There is a real danger that we treat God like *that person* in our lives. We like him, we love him, we enjoy his company, we value the relationship, but we always feel a little better if we have a backup plan, if we manage things on our own terms and hold onto control. We have never had cause to doubt him, of course, but we have had enough experience of disappointment with others to think, *Better safe than sorry.*

In the story of Abraham and Sarah, we have seen these great heroes of the faith do precisely this. They tried to fulfill God's promise of a child and family through their own scheming, thinking they would overcome Sarah's barrenness by taking her servant to be a wife for Abraham. We have seen Abraham trying to provide for his own protection by deceit: first in Egypt and then, 25 years later, again in the Negeb. But at every turn God has been patient to teach his servants that they can trust him fully and must wait upon him to do his work in his way.

In Genesis 21, God puts the final nail in the coffin of that way of relating to him and he shows them and us that we can trust him entirely, and that we *must* trust him. He shows us that he is faithful in every way. The faithfulness of God headlines the chapter. It is so clearly the theme right from the get-go: "The Lord visited Sarah as he had said, and the Lord did to Sarah as he had promised" (verse 1). This God is faithful. He is trustworthy. He can be relied upon. In our uncertain days, days of tremendous chaos and fearfulness, we need the reminder more than ever before. We see the faithfulness of God operating at two levels in this chapter, both in the practicalities of life and in the promise of salvation.

God's faithfulness in the practicalities of life

As a family, we used to live in England before moving to Canada. Like Canada, England has a state-funded health system—the National Health Service, or the NHS. It is often said of the NHS that it is a good system if you are really sick. If you have a life-threatening condition, you will get world-class care, but they are unlikely to take you seriously if you go in with a stubbed toe or a runny nose. We can fall into the trap of imagining that God is a bit like this stereotype of the NHS for us. We imagine that he will help us when we are knocking on eternity's door, but not if we have stubbed our toe. His interest in us and concern for us extend basically to getting us to heaven if we belong to Jesus. He will save us from the fires of judgment in the end, and we are certainly thankful for that, but as for the details of life in this world, we more or less need to fend for ourselves. We may not articulate things quite so starkly, but I think many of us slip into operating on those terms.

One of the great delights of this part of Abraham's story is that it highlights God's practical concern, his care and provision, for the family of faith. On the most basic level, we see God's provision in the fact that Abraham and Sarah can now resume family life. In chapter 20, they risked everything in the unwise dealings with Abimelech. Abraham could have lost Sarah. He could have faced the anger and murderous wrath of a pagan king for his deceit. It could have ended in complete tragedy. But here we are in chapter 21 and the story moves forward. Due to God's kindness, Abraham and Sarah still have each other, despite the sinful risks they took. How many times do we do things, even if not as dramatic as what Abraham did, and make unwise decisions that place ourselves and our loved ones at risk? Maybe a moral decision that could cost us dearly, a reckless financial decision or a decision to drive too fast when under time pressure. It could be any decision that, on reflection, was the wrong decision. We are spiritually naive if we do not look back and recognize the hand of God in protecting us each and every day. That is not to say he keeps us from every peril. Terrible things do happen, but God is actively involved in our care and protection all the time, and we cannot begin to imagine how many perils he has kept us from.

Abraham and Sarah reach this point as a family unit still intact, and that is due to the sheer kindness of God. Then we come to the gift of a child. There are huge salvation implications in Isaac's arrival. For now, let us consider the human and emotional aspects. Here is a couple that have been longing for a child for decades; no doubt, they have been crying out to the Lord to lift this burden of childlessness. In many cases, God does not choose to answer prayers of that kind in the ways we might hope, and some will know the pain of that. But in the gift of Isaac, we do see the tender care and compassion of God. After all these years, after all this heartache and waiting, "Sarah conceived and bore Abraham a son in his old age at the time of which God had spoken to him" (verse 2). This elderly couple could hardly believe the joy that was theirs; in fact, it brought laughter. They follow God's instructions and name the child Isaac, which means "he laughs" (verse 3). And it is laughable, joyfully so. Remember that Abraham is 100 years old at this point. Sarah exclaims: "God has made laughter for me; everyone who hears will laugh over me... Who would have said to Abraham that Sarah would nurse children? Yet I have borne him a son in his old age" (verses 6–7). Now this old couple have the joy of throwing a baby shower. Maybe some of their friends and contemporaries are pushing walkers rather than baby carriages when they arrive for the party. It has come about 75 years later than expected, but the party is on.

We need to recognize God's kindness, his compassion, and his faithfulness in all this. Abraham and Sarah had a big role in God's salvation plan that stretched well beyond themselves and their lifetime. But they were also ordinary human beings with longings and griefs and burdens of heart. God's kindness to them reminds us that he is faithful in his care for his children. He remembers us, he sees our tears and hears our cries, and has this heart of compassion toward us. That is not to say he will fulfill every longing in this life. But he is faithful and kind in his provision.

The story takes what feels like a darker turn in the midst of the celebration. In the joyful hubbub of the party, Sarah catches something out of the corner of her eye. It turns out that she was not the only one laughing at this turn of events. Her joyful laughter is echoed by a mocking laughter:

> "But Sarah saw the son of Hagar the Egyptian, whom she had borne to Abraham, laughing. So, she said to Abraham, 'Cast out this slave woman with her son, for the son of this slave woman shall not be heir with my son Isaac'" (verses 9–10).

Abraham is not keen to honor that request, but the Lord tells him to go ahead and do it. At the same time, he adds a provision of kindness. Yes, Isaac is the heir through whom the promises will come, but God also says: "I will make a nation of the son of the slave woman also, because he is your offspring" (verse 13).

On the morning of Hagar and Ishmael's departure, Abraham gets up early, no doubt with a heavy heart. He prepares a skin of water and some bread, gives it to Hagar and sends her away with the boy. We can just imagine all the emotions within Abraham's heart that morning: guilt, sadness, conflicted loyalty, regret. The wilderness of Beersheba is a tough environment, inhospitable, dry, and sparse in terms of vegetation or cover. Soon enough, predictably, the water is gone. Hagar puts her son under some bushes to shield him from the sun. The scene now is heart-rending: "Then she went and sat down opposite him, a good way off, about the distance of a bowshot, for she said, 'Let me not look on the death of the child'" (verse 16). Evidently both mother and child are crying out in fear and despair. It is a tragic scene of vulnerability and isolation. But verses 17 and 18 are beautiful:

> "And God heard the voice of the boy, and the angel of God called to Hagar from heaven and said to her, 'What troubles you, Hagar? Fear not, for God has heard the voice of the boy where he is. Up! Lift up the boy, and hold him fast with your hand, for I will make him into a great nation.'"

God heard. He saw. No one else was there to help. They were totally alone… Perhaps that is your situation at the moment: isolated, and vulnerable, and in need. Does anyone see? Does anyone hear? God does. He sees every vulnerability. He hears every cry. What a thought. What a truth. He hears and sees Hagar, extending his kindness in a special way out of faithfulness to his promises to Abraham. This is very interesting. God had indicated his intention in verse 13 that he would make a nation of Ishmael purely because he is Abraham's offspring. Hagar and Ishmael have now left the covenant household. Later, Hagar seeks for a wife for him from Egypt, not from the people of God. They are not inside the realm of God's salvation. It seems that they have stepped away. But God is still showing his kindness to them, expanding our view of his faithful concern.

Some of us are in that tough situation of seeing children or grandchildren who have walked away from the faith that they were once taught. They are off in the wilderness. No doubt it burdens and grieves you. In the midst of that concern, do not imagine that God does not care about them anymore. This scene in the wilderness is a lovely picture of how God's faithful care follows people, even as they travel away from the household of faith. He has not forgotten them. Obviously, we must pray for their salvation—the story is not telling us that God's eternal salvation reaches every wanderer—but it does remind us about the practical kindness God shows, even to the wanderer.

> "God opened [Hagar's] eyes, and she saw a well of water. And she went and filled the skin with water and gave the boy a drink. And God was with the boy, and he grew up. He lived in the wilderness and became an expert with the bow" (verses 19–20).

The Lord made a way for this family, this mother and son. He made a future for Ishmael, gave him gifts and skills and, in earthly terms, blessed him. And it shows us something of the faithfulness and kindness of God that almost seems to overflow from the household of faith and reach even to the wilderness.

We see another aspect of God's kindness and grace, just briefly, at the end of the chapter. You will remember how Abraham got into hot water with Abimelech in the previous chapter. Abraham deceived him, and almost caused Abimelech to fall under the immediate judgment of God. Abraham got there because he feared what this unbelieving Gentile king might do to him as he traveled through the land he controlled. But what happens here is quite wonderful. Abimelech notices that this Israelite enjoys the blessing of God. He has something special about him, and rather than resent that or want to persecute Abraham or drive him out, Abimelech is drawn to Abraham. In fact, he seems to have a kind of fearful respect for him:

> "At that time Abimelech and Phicol the commander of his army said to Abraham, 'God is with you in all that you do. Now therefore swear to me here by God that you will not deal falsely with me or with my descendants or with my posterity, but as I have dealt kindly with you, so you will deal with me and with the land where you have sojourned.' And Abraham said, 'I will swear'" (verses 22–24).

Abraham was shown favor and he and this Gentile king made a covenant. Just notice how it all ends: "Abraham planted a tamarisk tree in Beersheba and called there on the name of the Lord, the Everlasting God. And Abraham sojourned many days in the land of the Philistines" (verses 33–34). The Lord so worked in the situation and in the heart of this king that Abraham was given peace and liberty to worship the Lord and to dwell for many days in the land of the Philistines. The Lord took a potentially ugly situation—a relationship that started off on completely the wrong foot—and made a way for Abraham in this new land, among people who might have been his enemies. In the details and in the practicalities of life, God shows himself faithful.

The big challenges of faith are not always to do with believing that God will save us in the end from the fires of hell and welcome us into his eternal kingdom. Often the big challenges of faith focus in on the practicalities of life in this world. Those are so often the things we fret over and the things that stretch our faith the most. *Will God be with me, and go before me, as I move to a new place and start in a new job? Will he watch over my children and my loved ones? Can I trust him in my new season of uncertainty with health or finances? Can I rest in his grace in the midst of a family situation that threatens to unravel? Will he be faithful in all this?* Of course, there is no promise that God will spare us all grief and all loss, but this account shows us the depth and breadth of the loving care and faithfulness of God in the practicalities of life in this world. He has his finger on the details. He goes before us. He hears the cry and sees the distress, even of those living in the wilderness. What are the worries on your heart today for the practicalities of your life and the lives of your loved ones? Do you trust him in those things? Will you trust him to be faithful in the unknown challenges of the future?

God's faithfulness in the promise of salvation

There is, of course, something bigger going on here than the dramas of one man and his family, living at one point in ancient history, in one particular corner of the world. Right at the start of the Abraham story in Genesis 12, God made it clear that the story of this family would be painted on the wider canvas of world history and of salvation history. Abraham's life and future would be about the blessing of God coming to a broken world, part of the bigger drama of the Fall and of God's plan to make all things new:

> "I will make of you a great nation, and I will bless you and make your name great, so that you will be a blessing. I will bless those who bless you, and him who dishonors you I will curse, and in you all the families of the earth shall be blessed" (12:2–3).

As the story has progressed, the great barrier to the plan of God was the childlessness of Abraham and Sarah. They made a variety of missteps in thinking that the burden was on them to find an alternative solution to their crisis of infertility, but God continually reaffirmed his promise to give this couple a child. After the mess of chapter 16, God made it clear that his plan was unchanged: "Sarah your wife shall bear you a son, and you shall call his name Isaac. I will establish my covenant with him as an everlasting covenant for his offspring after him" (Genesis 17:19). The plan has been a long time in coming to fruition, but it has never deviated. And so, we reach chapter 21, "The Lord visited Sarah as he had said, and the Lord did to Sarah as he had promised. And Sarah conceived and bore Abraham a son in his old age at the time of which God had spoken to him" (verses 1–2).

As we read that statement, we recognize how familiar this storyline is for us as New Testament people. The plan of God comes to a point of fruition when the Lord brings a child to a woman in the most unlikely circumstances, to a woman who should not be expecting a baby. He does so by a miraculous intervention and in accordance with his Word. We have seen it before. Our mind turns quickly to Mary and Joseph and their startling news all those centuries later. And in this ancient moment of fulfilment of God's promise, we see a pointer to the greater fulfilment yet to come. God will bring salvation just as he promised—through Abraham's son, Isaac, in the first instance—but ultimately, through his Greater Son to come, the Lord Jesus Christ. Here in Genesis 21, the promised child—the baby of miraculous conception—stands center stage. God's purposes and God's plans revolve around him. It is the importance and centrality of this child within the salvation plan of God that ultimately makes sense of the narrative.

Do you find it a little strange or jarring that Hagar and her young son are sent away? It seems a little bit harsh, and we have some sympathy with Abraham when he is reluctant to follow through. We wonder why God seems for the plan. We will only make sense of this when we see that the promised baby Isaac is at the heart of all that is going on here. There is much rejoicing at Isaac's birth, a grand celebration. But there is that fly in the ointment when Sarah sees Ishmael laughing (verse 9). Sarah calls for Hagar and Ishmael to be thrown out. Abraham is upset: "And the thing was very displeasing to Abraham on account of his son" (verse 11). Sarah looks wrong here, and Abraham looks right. That is how most of us will read this. But that is not how God seems to see it and that is a bit of a surprise: "But God said to Abraham, 'Be not displeased because of the boy and because of your slave woman. Whatever Sarah says to you, do as she tells you'" (verse 12). Of course, the boy should not have been mean-spirited or mocking toward Isaac, but this seems like an over-reaction, and Abraham doubtless had a sense of real affection for Ishmael. In a time when children were less certain to live through infancy and childhood than they are today, perhaps this elderly father thought it was not such a bad idea having two sons in the house.

Why is it right for Hagar and Ishmael to go? Notice the reason God gives at the end of verse 12: do whatever Sarah says, "for through Isaac shall your offspring be named." The promise, the blessing, the covenant, the salvation plan, are going to come through Isaac. You do not need, and should not keep, a second son in the household. Ishmael is not the plan, and he never will be. More than that, Ishmael's response and reaction to the promised child actually sets him outside the blessings of the household. Isaac is God's miraculous gift to Abraham and Sarah. He is the means by which God will bring his blessing to the world. Yet Ishmael has shown, even in his youth, that his heart is set against the child of promise. And so, he is to go.

The coming of Isaac and departure of Ishmael teaches us two vitally important truths. It teaches us, on the one hand, that God will save in his way, by his appointed means, and in accordance with his spoken word. He will do it without the help or scheming of human agents. Ishmael came as a backup plan, from Abraham and Sarah's scheming. His departure is a sadness, but it is also a confirmation that God's salvation will come on his terms and not on human terms. In addition, the departure of Ishmael teaches us that access to salvation blessings is tied to our response to the miraculous child of promise. Ishmael and Hagar were sent away (which was costly for this young mother and her son) *because* Ishmael despised the promised child who would become the means of God's salvation. That was the trigger for it all.

As we stand back from all this, it leaves us with a question and a challenge. Will we take God at his word and trust in his promised salvation? Will we delight in the child of his promise? The default mode of the human heart is a works-based religion, a do-it-yourself approach to salvation. Thanks to YouTube, we are all becoming do-it-yourself home renovation experts, mechanics, plumbers, you name it. But we need to admit that there are certain things we simply cannot achieve on our own. Our salvation is one of them. Ishmael represented Abraham and Sarah's attempt to do God's work for him. And his dramatic exit from the story is a stark reminder that spiritual do-it-yourself solutions always fail. God's plan is to save us his own way—through the life, death, and resurrection of his promised child—to make us his very own. We need to see how seriously God takes our response to the promised child. We cannot have a home with God, or be part of his family or enjoy his blessings, if we will not welcome and receive his Son. So many in our world scorn and despise him; they mock him and reject him. The casting out of Hagar and Ishmael is a warning that God will not welcome those who do not welcome his Son.

God is the God of total faithfulness. He is faithful in his care and provision for his people. He is faithful in working out his plan of salvation as he promised through his Son. Will we take him at his word? Will we trust him today, and for the days that are to come?

11

The Lord who provides

Genesis 22

Sometimes we find ourselves needing to develop skills that we did not particularly want to possess. Anyone who moves to Canada from elsewhere needs to learn some skills of winter survival, whether they like it or not. If you drive a car, you need to figure out how to drive in the snow. You might not enjoy it, but you had better figure out how to do it. When our family lived in London, I traveled to work by train and had to learn the key London survival skill, which is to contort yourself into the remaining sliver of space on a completely packed commuter train, ensuring that your whole body and laptop bag are clear of the closing door, holding your breath until the door is sealed shut, and exhaling only when the train begins to move. It was not a skill I wanted to acquire, but I got pretty good at it; there was really no choice.

In the Christian life, whether we like it or not, if we are going to walk with the Lord, *we need to learn how to endure trial.* With the Lord's help, we need to figure out what it looks like to walk through seasons of testing. We would never choose those seasons willingly, but the hard reality is that they will come, and we will be called to live through them. For all of us, the question of how we will persevere must be addressed. For some, this is an urgent question, because God has called you to walk through a particular trial at the moment. He is testing your faith today, and so the question is a pressing one: How do I walk with God through seasons of trial and of testing?

We come to Genesis 22 and perhaps the most dramatic test that God ever calls one of his servants to endure. Notice how the chapter begins:

> "After these things God *tested Abraham* and said to him, 'Abraham!' And he said, 'Here I am.' He said, 'Take your son, your only son Isaac, whom you love, and go to the land of Moriah, and offer him there as a burnt offering on one of the mountains of which I shall tell you'" (verses 1–2, my emphasis).

You will remember that Abraham and Sarah have just experienced the Lord's kindness in a very wonderful way. They have faced childlessness for decades. For a quarter century and more, they have had the promise of God ringing in their ears that they would have a child. And now, finally, with Abraham having reached the grand old age of 100, the Lord has fulfilled his promise and given them the long-awaited son. Genesis 21 ended on a very happy note for this elderly couple. They are enjoying the fulfilment of the promise of God. They are enjoying the protection of God. Having made a covenant of friendship with the king in their region, they are free to live as a family under the blessing of God. It is a situation of domestic and spiritual bliss. But having experienced the blessing of God in this way, God calls Abraham into a time of testing. Right there is a lesson for us. The life of faith has different seasons. There will be times of ease, times when the Lord brings us into a pleasant place. But in his wisdom and providence, he rarely leaves us in those situations for too long without disruption. That is certainly the case for Abraham here. God tells him that he is to take his son, who is the precious child of the promise, and sacrifice him as a burnt offering. As we read those words, we pause in shock and even horror. We can scarcely imagine what Abraham must have thought and how he must have felt.

This is, of course, a very moving and a very challenging account. It is an account of God calling his follower, his friend, his servant, to endure a very terrible test. Within it, we learn deep truths that will teach us, if we will listen, how it is that we may walk with God through times of testing and trial. I want to enter into the narrative and look at it from two angles: I want us to see how this test reveals and demonstrates Abraham's outstanding model of faith, and at the same time how it reveals the marvelous provision of God.

Abraham's model of faith

True character often emerges under pressure. Some of our greatest leaders in history showed their true mettle under pressure. A little while ago, some controversy arose over the decision to remove the bust of Winston Churchill from the Oval Office of the White House. Churchill is revered on both sides of the Atlantic for his extraordinary leadership during the Second World War. In peacetime, one might argue that Churchill was less of an effective leader, but in the fire and fear of war, he was extraordinary by any measure. Without his leadership, we might well question whether the Nazi menace could have been defeated, and we might wonder how very different the world could look today.

If true character often emerges under pressure, it is also the case that true convictions are often shown in the furnace of difficulty. Without doubt, *true faith* is often revealed in the kiln of testing, trial, and adversity. I have seen that again and again in the lives of believers when they suffer. If you want to know the true worth and depth of a believer's faith, do not watch them so much in a time of ease, seek them out and observe them in a time of testing. It is actually a tremendous privilege to be near to a mature disciple of Christ when they go through the fire of adversity or the agony of loss. This is when you will discover what they really believe and what they are really made of in spiritual terms. It can be a truly wonderful thing just to observe. That is very much the case with Abraham here. Abraham had plenty of low points in his discipleship and plenty of failures, but his mature faith is on full display here.

Try to imagine yourself in Abraham's shoes. Having waited decades for this promised child, who eventually arrives by nothing short of a divine miracle, the Lord comes to him and says: *Go and sacrifice your son on an altar.* The reasonable thing would surely be to protest and refuse. This instruction goes against every instinct as a parent. It seems to go against what Abraham knows of the Lord's will and his purposes. But what does Abraham do? It is so very striking:

> "So Abraham rose early in the morning, saddled his donkey, and took two of his young men with him, and his son Isaac. And he cut wood for the burnt offering and arose and went to the place of which God had told him" (verse 3).

When God speaks in this chapter, Abraham listens, Abraham follows, and Abraham obeys. That is the big emphasis here. It is a pattern throughout the account. God speaks in verse 2, and Abraham immediately sets out: "to the place of which God had told him." Here is a servant of God walking into what looks like a complete disaster of a situation, but he does it because God has spoken, and because he takes God at his word.

That is a very challenging path of discipleship. God has said a great deal to us in his Word, and following often looks costly and painful. Often it *will* be costly and painful. The Lord calls us to forsake ourselves, to take up our cross and follow him. He calls us to stand out from our world and our culture in countless ways: to reject sin, to profess Christ, and to speak his truth. In our age, these are hard and costly things to do. In the situation at work where your boss asks you to cover a lie, to sign off on a falsehood, and the Word of God calls you to refuse, obedience might be very costly. In the situation at university where your professor asks for your view on a moral issue, or on some aspect of your worldview or anthropology or ethic, and you have to decide whether to stand on God's Word or capitulate to culture and say what your professor wants to hear, obedience might cost you. In the situation with friends, when they are doing something you know is wrong, and acceptance will mean joining in, you have to decide whether to obey God's Word, or fit in with the crowd. You know in the moment of decision that obedience will be costly.

Listening to God's voice and obeying his Word can lead us in a direction that is frankly scary, toward consequences that make us wince. Nothing, of course, that God calls us to is more challenging than the call Abraham received. Yet, he trusted. He followed. He obeyed. We have to ask, why did he do that? How was he able to do it? The model of faith is wonderful but, if we want to understand and emulate it, we need to know what it was that Abraham saw, understood, and believed.

As the story moves forward, it becomes clear that God gave Abraham faith and insight to trust in some quite specific ways. Verse 5 is really very interesting. Abraham and his men approach the mountain of sacrifice, and Abraham tells them, "Stay here with the donkey; I and the boy will go over there and worship and come again to you." Abraham has been told to slaughter his son. He evidently believes that he will do so, and yet he tells his traveling companions that he and the boy will come back, as in fact they do. Why does Abraham say that? *How* can he say that? He clearly intends to follow through on the instruction. He believes that the boy will die. It might be tempting to assume that Abraham was not being quite honest with them. He knew the boy was not coming back, but he could not admit that much at that stage, and so he undertakes a little *massaging* of the truth. He is not quite honest, but we almost understand. However, that is *not* what is taking place here, and the writer of Hebrews makes that clear for us:

> "By faith Abraham, when he was tested, offered up Isaac, and he who had received the promises was in the act of offering up his only son, of whom it was said, 'Through Isaac shall your offspring be named.' He considered that God was able even to raise him from the dead, from which, figuratively speaking, he did receive him back" (Hebrews 11:17–19).

When Abraham was tested, he had faith. In particular, he had faith in God's covenant promise that he would make a great nation of him, and through his family, bring blessing to the world. Isaac was the key to the fulfilment of that promise. God had made that clear. So, what did Abraham reason by faith when God called upon him to sacrifice Isaac? He reasoned that God must be planning to bring him back from the dead, because there was no way that Isaac could die and stay dead, and the promise of God be fulfilled. *And anyway,* he thought, *the Sovereign God is more than able to overcome the grave.*

Here is the great insight, here is what Hebrews reveals. Abraham says to the guys, *Look, Isaac and I are going up the mountain for a bit. We are taking a hike but don't worry, we will both be back soon.* He was not fibbing or massaging the truth, but rather he was making a declaration of faith in the covenant promise of God and in the life-giving power of God. He had no idea why God was allowing him to go through this trial. He had no idea exactly how all this would play out. But he believed the covenant promise. He did not know the details, but he knew the big picture.

If we belong to Jesus by faith, we have the covenant promises of God. We know the outcome of God's story because we have it in God's Word. We do not know the details of how our trial will end or of how our crisis will be resolved, but we know that God will save his people. We know that he will make us like his Son. We know that death can never be the end for us. We know that God has resurrection power. We know that he will take us home. We know that we have a secure future in a new heaven and a new earth. And so, we can walk into trial and stand up under testing because we know that the promises of God cannot fail. That is powerful fuel for faith in the face of trial. If God will keep all his promises to me, if death is no barrier to him, if my future is secure, then what trial is enough to sink my faith? What trial can truly unsettle me? That is what Abraham knew and believed, and it is why he put one foot in front of the other and went to that mountain.

Abraham and Isaac go up the mountain, Isaac carrying the wood of the sacrifice and Abraham carrying the fire and knife. Isaac innocently asks the obvious question in verse 7: "Behold, the fire and the wood, but where is the lamb for a burnt offering?" Abraham replies, "God will provide for himself the lamb for a burnt offering, my son." *Abraham, how can you trick your son like that? Does he not deserve the truth? You are planning to place him on an altar and plunge a knife into his flesh. How can you live with such a lie on top of everything else?* We do not know what kind of insight the Lord gave Abraham, but his assurance to Isaac was more true than perhaps he knew. It is worth remembering at this point that the Lord has recently called Abraham a prophet, the first prophet of the Bible (20:7). It seems there is some prophetic insight here. The Lord has given him an inkling of something, some flash of insight. Faith in God's promises, his power, and his plan enabled Abraham to press forward in this dreadful act of obedience.

We might look at Abraham as a great hero of faith, who went through a test that was unusually tough, and then reason that we cannot all be like Abraham, and probably should not try. It is true enough; Abraham's role was special and his test was unusual. But if we have learned anything from recent chapters, it is that Abraham was profoundly fallible and remarkably weak, just like us. It is also worth remembering that our privilege is in some ways much greater than his. Abraham believed that God would provide the Lamb, *but he had not met the Savior who would come*. He believed that God had life-giving power, *but he had not witnessed the resurrection of Christ*. Unlike him, we look back on the fulfilment of these promises. We look back to Calvary in history and in Scripture, whereas Abraham only looked forward through a darkened lens. We look back to that first Easter with confidence, whereas Abraham took refuge in simple hope. We have something that Abraham did not have. In Abraham's faith, there is a true model for trusting God in trial and enduring through even the hardest test.

For a few years in my twenties while I was finishing off my studies, I worked as a schoolteacher in London. One of my responsibilities was leading an outdoor expedition program. For each trip, we had to fill out lengthy risk assessments for every activity we planned. The need for sensible risk assessments is obvious but, to be honest, they became a little bit tedious and slightly absurd at points. But as I reflect on writing those rather dull assessments, I think of Abraham and his test of faith. It strikes me that when it comes to the life of faith, Abraham's outlook is so different from an overly risk-averse and cautious outlook. *God says to do it, so I will; and I will leave the risks and the costs to him.* Now, that is faith—simple, radical, uncalculating faith. It is the only way to live the Christian life, the only way to walk through testing and to endure under trial. If we are obsessed with avoiding risk and cost, we are going to have a tough time following the Lord wherever he may lead. Where is God calling you to tear up the risk assessment, to take him at his word, and to walk with him through the darkness, with your hand in his?

God's marvelous provision

The focus now moves away from Abraham and the faith lessons he teaches us, and the beam shines on God and the provision he makes. The scene has been set. There is tension in the air. We are anticipating a great tragedy. There is a big part of us that wants to turn our eyes away at this moment. Abraham is plodding on obediently by faith, but we feel nervous. The thought of the death of a child, the thought that the father himself might sink in the blade and light the match is too awful to contemplate. The story may be familiar, but try to picture the scene with me and imagine the events unfold:

> "When they came to the place of which God had told him, Abraham built the altar there and laid the wood in order and bound Isaac his son and laid him on the altar, on top of the wood. Then Abraham reached out his hand and took the knife to slaughter his son" (verses 9–10).

The tension is now at the highest point. The blade is lifted above the boy, his father grasping the handle with both hands, no doubt quivering with an awful sense of expectancy and grief.

And just as Abraham steels himself for the act that would go against every fiber of his being and devastate his heart, the angel of the Lord calls out to him from heaven: "Abraham, Abraham!" *Do not harm the boy. Don't do anything to him,* "for now I know that you fear God, seeing you have not withheld your son, your only son from me" (verse 12). Abraham looks up, and sees a ram caught in the thicket and he offers the ram as a burnt offering instead of his son.

In that moment, Abraham sees how the Lord had it all planned out. He sees that the Lord did indeed have an offering prepared. He was proved right in his trust in the Lord and in his prophetic pronouncements of what the Lord would do. Abraham marked the Lord's provision and marked the occasion by naming the place, "'The Lord will provide'; as it is said to this day, 'On the mountain of the Lord it shall be provided'" (verse 14). "The Lord will provide,"—or "Jehovah Jireh" in the old King James Version. Evidently it became a saying, repeated down through the years, "On the mountain of the Lord it shall be provided."

We are told at the beginning of the chapter that the Lord sent Abraham to the land of Moriah for this test. The place where the father was called upon to offer his son—and the place where the Lord made provision—was a mount in Moriah. Scholars identify this as the region where Jerusalem would be built. It is possible that this mount is the very mount on which the temple was built, where all those animal sacrifices would be given down through the years. It is possible, too, that this mount was another mount, just outside the city. A mount to which another Son of another Father carried the wood of his altar. The mount upon which another Son was called to die, even perishing at the will of his Father. As we consider that, and as we look at the Lord's choreography of all this—his planning and the powerful symbolism—it really is enough to send a shiver down the spine. As ever, it is worthwhile to stand back and ask what is the larger significance of this drama. Why does God do this? Why does he allow it? As we have seen again and again in the story of Abraham, his own story and the story of his family is about much more than him, and much more than them. They are part of the grander story of God's plan to redeem a broken world and bless a lost world and to do so through his seed, his line, through his coming great descendant. This time of testing and this terrible drama is about that bigger story of God's great salvation plan.

The death of a child is an unspeakable thing for any parent to have to endure. I know some who have endured that very thing, and I can only begin to imagine the heart-rending agony. It is a parent's worst nightmare, and I think it must be the cruelest pain that this stricken world can inflict on anyone. Abraham is the one at the center of God's plan to overcome the curse of sin and death in this world. It is quite something that God calls him to face the prospect of this deepest of trials and this ugliest of agonies, and to come so very near to the reality of it. In sparing Abraham the experience in the end, in making a saving provision and sparing Isaac's young life, the Lord is saying something wonderful here. He is pointing to something profound. When the Lord Jesus arrives on the scene, all those centuries later, John the Baptist famously says of him, "Behold, the Lamb of God, who takes away the sin of the world" (John 1:29). Jesus comes to be the Lamb, the sacrifice, says John. Jesus comes as the Son of the Father, the beloved and only Son. At the transfiguration, the Father declares of the Son, "This is my beloved Son; listen to him" (Mark 9:7). But then, as this Son nears the place of execution, in obedience to the Father's will, there is no final change of plan. There is no alternative introduced. As the Son hangs upon the cross, he cries out to the Father, "My God, my God, why have you forsaken me?" (Mark 15:34).

God called Abraham to walk toward the worst trial imaginable in this fallen world: to lose his beloved son, and even to participate in his death. But at the final moment God shows that he will provide a substitute. He will provide the lamb. And at the cross of Calvary—perhaps even at the same location as Abraham's test—God the Father gives his Son to die as the substitute for his beloved children. Jesus enters into the suffering and agony of life in this world, he plumbs its depth and pays its price. Jesus teaches us with a depth of meaning that Abraham could not see in full detail in his day, but saw from a distance, that the Lord would indeed provide. The Lord would provide the substitute to die so that none of Abraham's family, the family of faith, would ever face the ultimate death. He would provide the great sacrifice for sin, so that the wreckage of the Fall might be undone for those who believe. The Lord would provide and show himself to be Jehovah Jireh.

I want to go back to this idea of trial and the theme of testing. I do not think it is incidental to the story. There is a grand lesson here about the Lord's provision that speaks to us and touches our hearts in times of trial. God called Abraham to face the worst thing anyone could face. He brought him under the most grueling test anyone could endure. And in the midst of that trial and test, he painted a prophetic, symbol-laden picture of what he, the Father, would do for Abraham and for Isaac and for the entire family of faith. For those under trial, we need to know that the God who sometimes sees fit to test us and try us is the God who entered into the drama of the worst of trials in the Person of his Son. He is the God who suffered as a man for us, who suffered profoundly, in our place. And this God, whose ways we will not always understand, has provided all that we need at Calvary. He will provide all that we need for today. He meets you in your need—your need for rescue, for forgiveness, and for salvation. The God who made that provision for you will not abandon you in your need today.

As Paul says in Romans 8:32, "He who did not spare his own Son but gave him up for us all, how will he not also with him graciously give us all things?"

I do not know what trial you are facing today. I do not know what test you may need to endure tomorrow. But I know this: the God who gave his beloved only Son for us on the mount of crucifixion is not the God who stands far off, unmoved. He truly is the Lord who provides, and if you will trust him in the darkness, and lean upon his Word, you will know and discover for yourself that he is indeed "Jehovah Jireh, the Lord who provides."

12

Waiting for a homeland

Genesis 23

It seemed that Abraham and Sarah must have drunk from a fountain of eternal youth. When we met them at the beginning of their great story, they were already pretty elderly. Too elderly, we might think, to begin a great adventure, and far too elderly to start a family. However, God met them and made promises to them—promises of blessing in a land of curse and of salvation in a world under judgment. Abraham and Sarah represented a new start and a new story in this sin-stricken world. They would be the channels of life and hope. God gave this elderly and childless couple the gift of a son in their extreme old age as a living and breathing symbol of that hope. There is something about Abraham and Sarah as recipients and channels of the blessing of God that seems to defy gravity when it comes to age and physical decline and the pull of the grave.

In Genesis 23, the pull of mortal gravity wins out, and the grave claims Sarah. Although we knew it was coming, we find it all a bit jarring and unsettling and sad. The image of Abraham's tears of mourning for his wife of so many decades makes for a moving and a tragic scene in verse 2. At the same time, it is here to instruct us and encourage us. As we have seen so often through their story, Abraham's and Sarah's lives have a wider meaning. They are recipients and conduits of the great promises of God: promises that counteract the judgment of Genesis 3, that constitute the nation of Israel, and that point to Christ and our salvation in him.

As we reflect upon the death of Sarah, we need to consider her passing within the bigger picture of these promises of God. Abraham's next words give us something of a key. Notice what he does and what he says:

> "And Abraham rose up from before his dead and said to the Hittites, 'I am a sojourner and foreigner among you; give me property among you for a burying place, that I may bury my dead out of my sight'" (verses 3–4).

As a semi-nomadic person, Abraham has no land on which to bury his dead and so he must go to the local landowners and ask. As he does so, he summarizes his situation: he is a sojourner and a foreigner. A sojourner is a person who is passing through, someone on a journey who may spend time in a given place but does not have a permanent home there. That is what Abraham is and what Sarah has been—a sojourner and foreigner. To us, that might look as though something along the way went wrong, some element of God's plan failed and fell short. There is something in this that feels unsatisfactory or disappointing. Surely, they could have had *more* or might have expected *more*. But the rest of Scripture does not see it that way. The New Testament would point to Abraham and Sarah's status as sojourners and foreigners in the land as a model for the rest of us.[1] The New Testament would tell us that every true believer must live as they did in that key respect. As they were sojourners and foreigners in their day, so too must we be in ours.

Sojourners and foreigners hold lightly to their earthly home

Abraham and Sarah had left their homeland many decades before. God had called them to leave their family and familiar territory and go to the place where he would send them: a land he would give to their descendants. They duly packed up, departed, and so began a lifestyle of wandering. They became semi-nomads, going to the land of promise, but not settling in any city, not buying land or building a house, but rather moving from place to place as so many keepers of herds and flocks would likewise have done. That lifestyle certainly left them vulnerable in some ways. We saw that vulnerability in their interactions with King Abimelech back in Genesis 20. The land was theirs by divine promise, but it was not yet theirs by geo-political reality.

Some of us have always lived in the same house, others have moved around a lot. We have a number of military families in our church, and families with a parent in the armed forces tend to know something about moving around. Ministry families and missionaries often know that too. Looking back at our own family's story, we had five different homes in our first ten years of marriage, and I remember the conversations and the questions we turned over in our mind: *When do we stop moving and settle down in one place?* Maybe you have an experience of that kind. Maybe you are a wanderer and a pilgrim in that sense even now.

As the years have gone by and Abraham and Sarah have continued on their pilgrimage, we might have imagined that the Lord would have given them space and opportunity to settle down, to build a homestead or establish a community, to put down roots. But that is not what happened. We reach the end of Sarah's life and discover that she is still rootless. She never built that dream home. She and Abraham never got to sit down with the architect to imagine and draw, or to choose fittings, fixtures, and paint colors with the interior decorator. Adding to the sadness of Sarah's passing, we see her elderly husband having to go to the city gate, among foreigners, to secure a place to bury her.

It is one thing to die at home, among your own people, maybe even in the house where you lived with your family. Death is always a sadness, but there is comfort there. Yet to die in a foreign land, among people who are not your people, that is harder. If a family goes on a journey and suffers a bereavement while they are away, as sometimes happens, it is a particularly hard grief to bear. There is something especially tragic about it. We sense something of the difficulty of this situation as Abraham collects himself and considers his next steps:

> "And Abraham rose up from before his dead and said to the Hittites, 'I am a sojourner and foreigner among you; give me property among you for a burying place, that I may bury my dead out of my sight'" (verses 3–4).

Abraham cuts a lonely figure, rising up from before *his dead*. No one knows his grief as he knows it. He goes not before his family and kinsmen, but before the Hittites and declares this obvious truth: "I am a sojourner and a foreigner among you." The New Testament makes it clear that this is at the core of what Abraham teaches us about the life of faith. The writer of Hebrews really drives the point home:

> "By faith Abraham obeyed when he was called to go out to a place that he was to receive as an inheritance. And he went out, not knowing where he was going. By faith he went to live in the land of promise, as in a foreign land, living in tents with Isaac and Jacob, heirs with him of the same promise. For he was looking forward to the

> city that has foundations, whose designer and builder is God" (Hebrews 11:8–10).

Why were Abraham and Sarah willing to live as semi-nomads all those years? They were clearly wealthy enough to settle down. Why live in tents all that time, even when they were in the land of promise, the land God was giving them? They lived that way because they were looking forward to the city of God—the city that has foundations, the heavenly city, where their true home lies. The writer goes on, thinking of Abraham and Sarah and perhaps other heroes of faith:

> "These all died in faith, not having received the things promised, but having seen them and greeted them from afar, and having acknowledged that they were strangers and exiles on the earth. For people who speak thus make it clear that they are seeking a homeland. If they had been thinking of that land from which they had gone out, they would have had opportunity to return. But as it is, they desire a better country, that is, a heavenly one. Therefore God is not ashamed to be called their God, for he has prepared for them a city" (Hebrews 11:13–16).

There is a way of life that characterizes the true people of God. People who have faith and trust God's promises "see" those promises and "greet them from afar." Such people live as strangers and exiles in the earth, as sojourners and foreigners, as people who are just passing through. There is deep challenge and rich encouragement for us here. There is deep challenge for us if we are making this world too much our home. There are all kinds of ways we may do that. We do it in terms of our values if we are not careful. The society around us does not know our Lord or esteem his Word, and the way and the way in which the people of God think and live is foreign to them. And it should be. We need to stick out like sore thumbs from those around us. We need to be recognizably different in how we view the world, in our ethics, in our priorities. We need to recognize the intense pressure we and our children are under to absorb and adopt the world's outlook. In the world into which I was born, it was probably seen as *quaint* to hold to Christian belief and a Christian ethic. Now in many quarters, Christianity is seen as something more sinister and subversive, a repressive set of values that needs to be dismantled and pushed aside. We have to ask ourselves with urgency: *Are we willing to live as sojourners and foreigners in this world when it comes to our values, ethics, and worldview?* It will mean discomfort and a real sense of being an outsider to live as one whose home is in another land.

We need to live as sojourners as well when it comes to our home and possessions. There is something very important to us about having a home and having our own things around us. There is nothing wrong with having a home and belongings. Abraham and Sarah were not poor; Abraham was able to produce what appeared to be a substantial amount of money to buy land as needed. Back in Genesis 13, he and Lot clearly had become so prosperous that they needed to separate to ensure enough land for their flocks and herds and growing households. It is not that Abraham and Sarah had nothing or lived in poverty or refused all earthly comfort. But as they walked with the Lord and followed him by faith, they did not place their security in putting down roots and securing their position in the community. That was not their outlook or priority. In that sense, they were somewhat otherworldly. We all love to build earthyly security and find earthly comfort. But for the people of God, there is a sense that our roots only ever go so deep here on this earth. Our danger is simply that, in seeking security and comfort in the world, we will place our hope in the life we have created for ourselves here—in our home, possessions, and wealth. Our danger is that if we settle too much into our earthly home, we will stop looking to our heavenly home.

The Lord calls his people to be sojourners—those who are just passing through. Let me ask you: If we really believed ourselves to be sojourners in this world and temporary tenants in our homes (not the eternal residents as we might sometimes imagine), what might change in our attitude to our possessions? Would we perhaps accumulate less? Would we perhaps be less concerned about savings and wealth? Would we be more ready to be generous and use what we have? Would we perhaps be a little less concerned about making everything perfect in our houses, keeping the décor 100 percent up-to-date, buying the very nicest gadgets and furnishings? Not that any of those things are bad in themselves, but maybe our drive to make our houses *just so* speaks to a heart issue, to the fact that we have forgotten that this world is not our home. Perhaps our desire for financial security speaks to a faith issue that forgets to hold lightly to our earthly wealth.

Sojourners and foreigners hope fully in God's promises

One of the hardest things about the Christian life is that we do not see the full outworking of God's plans and promises this side of the grave. We see indications and glimpses, and we see God at work, but so much is unfinished and unseen. Speaking of home, we have been doing a bit of redecorating and remodeling in our basement over recent months (and I know I need to remind myself to hold lightly to my earthly home in the midst of it…). Progress has been very slow. We reach a point where the job is half done. The tools are all out. There is dust and mess—and then I have to set aside the project for a few days because I am busy with other things. And we find ourselves constantly saying to one another: *When will this job ever be completed? We just want to see it finished and done.* We want to see the result.

We do have the satisfaction of seeing the end result of some of our earthly projects and undertakings, but the journey of faith is not like that. We live in hope of God's promises. We stake everything on his Word. We invest ourselves in serving him for as many years as he gives us. And then we die and are buried, and we trust and believe we will see the fruit the other side of the grave.

Sarah wandered with Abraham for decades in the journey of faith and went at his side to the land of promise, but she never saw her family take possession of one square inch of the land. Her husband had nowhere to bury her when she died. All those years of pilgrimage, and not even a burial plot in the Promised Land for her. If you were Abraham, what might you consider doing at this point? What would be your instinct? On some level, surely you would think, *We have been wandering all these years in this unfamiliar land, at the instruction of God. Now my wife has died and, as I lay her body in the dust of the earth, I would like to do that in my homeland. I would like to go back to the land of my fathers for this.* That is how many would feel. But what Abraham does is instructive—it speaks to his convictions. He goes to the landowners in the local city gate, where business was conducted. It may be that he needed a public exchange there because, as a foreigner, his land purchase needed collective approval. We do not quite know. But he goes before these foreigners, and it is interesting how the narrative highlights his precarious position, "Abraham rose and bowed to the Hittites, the people of the land" (verse 7).

It is their land, and Abraham makes an appeal to buy. As it turns out, they immediately respond that he can bury Sarah anywhere he likes, but he insists that he wants to purchase:

> "And he said to them, 'If you are willing that I should bury my dead out of my sight, hear me and entreat for me Ephron the son of Zohar, that he may give me the cave of Machpelah, which he owns; it is at the end of his field. For the full price let him give it to me in your presence as property for a burying place'" (verses 8–9).

Ephron says to Abraham, "No, I will give you the field. Do not worry about the cost" (verse 11). But Abraham insists. He wants to buy the land and own it, and he wants it to be a matter of public record that it is his: "And he said to Ephron in the hearing of the people of the land, 'But if you will, hear me: I will give the price of the field. Accept it from me, that I may bury my dead there'" (verse 13). Ephron continues to make polite noises about giving the land to him but just drops in the fact that it is worth 400 shekels of silver. It seems this was a great deal of money. Abraham immediately weighs out the money and hands it over. The deal closes and the title is registered in the eyes of the witnesses in the town:

> "So, the field of Ephron in Machpelah, which was to the east of Mamre, the field with the cave that was in it and all the trees that were in the field, throughout its whole area, was made over to Abraham as a possession in the presence of the Hittites, before all who went in at the gate of his city. After this, Abraham buried Sarah his wife in the cave of the field of Machpelah east of Mamre (that is, Hebron) in the land of Canaan. The field and the cave that is in it were made over to Abraham as a property for a burying place by the Hittites" (verses 17–20).

Most of this chapter has been given over to a real estate transaction following Sarah's death in verse 2. Abraham goes to some trouble to secure a burial plot. He is warmly invited just to take any place of his choosing, but he insists that he wants to buy land fair and square. Why? What is all this about?

Remember this is the Promised Land—the land God committed to give to Abraham's family as a tangible expression of his commitment to them. It signifies his promise to bless them, and make them a blessing, and to extend salvation blessings to the world through them. Thus far Abraham has not taken ownership of a square inch of that Promised Land. But he believes the promise, and he sees that this burial plot is significant—it is the down payment and the claim on the promise of God. If he were to pack up, go back to his father's land and bury Sarah there, it would be a faithless move. But securing this corner of the land and burying his wife there is a declaration that he believes that God is still committed to his promise and is still doing his work. It is fascinating how Abraham puts money behind that. He has never bothered to buy or build a house in all these years, but at this point, when he sees the symbolic necessity of securing the plot, money is no object. A substantial price is set and, without pausing for breath, Abraham counts out the cash. Why is he spending like this? Because, even if his family do not yet have a permanent dwelling place in the Promised Land, they will be laid to rest there as a mark of their faith that God will keep his promises to them. The cave in this field becomes a powerful symbol of the chosen family's hope in their inheritance. When Abraham dies in chapter 25, we are told that his sons bury him in this same place. When his grandson Jacob later dies in Egypt, his sons honor his request to be buried in Canaan:

> "Thus his sons did for him as he had commanded them, for his sons carried him to the land of Canaan, and buried him in the cave of the field at Machpelah, to the

> east of Mamre, which Abraham bought with the field from Ephron the Hittite to possess as a burying place" (50:12–13).

Genesis ends with Jacob's son Joseph dying in Egypt, but making his family swear to him that they will take his bones to the Promised Land to bury them there (50:25). What is the significance of all this? The people of God do not enter the fullness of the promises of God in this life, but they know that in death God will not fail them. The symbolism is so powerful. They *will* be buried in the right place because God is not done fulfilling his promises. The fulfilment of the promises of God is not all seen and experienced in this life, but his people know that the fulfilment will indeed come.

We need to learn this deep truth if we are to keep walking with the Lord in this life, where so much of what we hope for is yet unseen. The Lord Jesus may return tomorrow, of course, but if he does not return before we die, we will go to our graves not having seen the fulfilment of the great and glorious plans of God. We need to learn to be ok with that, to see with the eyes of faith what God has for us, and to greet those things from afar—even as Sarah did, even as Abraham did. We live in a world of instant gratification. If we want to know something, the knowledge of the world is on our phone in our pocket. If we want to buy something we cannot yet afford, the bank is all too ready to lend. If we want to watch something, anything, we can stream it in an instant. If we want to say something to the world, social media is ready to oblige. In a world that no longer knows how to wait for anything, we must be those who are content to wait for the great things before us—the coming of the kingdom, the resurrection of the body, the immediate presence of our Savior, and the complete absence of sin. These things are not our experience yet, but they will be. We live in hope, and we may well be buried in hope, but we learn from Sarah and from Abraham to place our hope fully in the promises of God. The picture of these believers of old being laid to rest in a particular tomb as a declaration of trust is very poignant. In a sense, it is the ultimate declaration of trust. *These bones of mine are being laid down in your place of promise, Lord, and I am trusting you that you will take care of the rest.*

My mind turns to another tomb in the same land: a tomb made available to another member of this same family who owned no land. He died trusting that the Father would fulfill his promise and complete his work. And the miracle is that on the third day this Son of Abraham was vindicated in his trust as the Father raised him to life again. Jesus promises resurrection life, fulfilment of the promises, and hope for the future to all who believe. His resurrection is the guarantee of every believer's resurrection. On a day yet to come, Sarah's body, laid in that tomb by Abraham, will be raised to resurrection life and she will walk into the fullness of the promises of God. She will do that because of her greater Son, the Lord Jesus Christ, who died for her, and who rose again. As we see the sweep of that promise and of what God intended to do, it takes our breath away and fills us with hope and joyful conviction to live in this world as Sarah did.

Sojourners and foreigners live honorably in society

It is noteworthy that Abraham was clearly held in high esteem by the Hittites where he lived. That really jumps off the page here. When Abraham goes before the men of the city, in need of a place to bury his wife, notice their response:

> "The Hittites answered Abraham, 'Hear us, my lord: you are a prince of God among us. Bury your dead in the choicest of our tombs. None of us will withhold

> from you his tomb to hinder you from burying your dead'" (verses 5–6).

That response speaks volumes about Abraham's reputation in the community. The way he conducts himself through this whole exchange is so polite, gracious, and full of integrity. He bows before them and speaks with respect and care. When they offer him free land, he insists on paying market price. At every turn, his behavior is impeccable. The Hittites could not fault him and evidently esteemed him. It seems entirely possible that Peter had all this in mind when he wrote these words:

> "Beloved, I urge you as *sojourners and exiles* to abstain from the passions of the flesh, which wage war against your soul. Keep your conduct among the Gentiles honorable, so that when they speak against you as evildoers, they may see your good deeds and glorify God on the day of visitation" (1 Peter 2:11–12, my emphasis).

Abraham knew something (or, we should say, *learned something,* because he was not always good at this) about living honorably among the Gentiles in the society in which God placed him. This is very significant in a chapter thinking about future hope, as we might fall into the error of imagining that our engagement with the society around us does not matter.

We Christians are guilty of this sometimes. We can be so discouraged and disgruntled with the world around us while we wait for heaven that we end up not being great neighbors or good participants in our society and community. If we are not careful, we can end up being someone that the local businessperson or politician or schoolteacher rather dreads seeing, because we are a bit difficult or grumpy, or just disengaged and unhelpful. That is not the way that people of faith live in this world. We are sojourners and foreigners, but we are to live honorably precisely because we know the Lord, treasure his promises, and have a hope that stretches well beyond this world. "I am a sojourner and foreigner among you," says Abraham. May the Lord help us to see ourselves that way and to honor him as we pass through life in this world, on our way to our true and lasting home.

13

The blessing continues

Genesis 24:1–25:18

Most of us have rather a short attention span. We get into a new hobby or a new job, and we are all energy and enthusiasm. We feel this is *the* big thing for us now, our life's passion. We are going to give it 100 percent. Then inevitably, we soon get bored and lose interest. Our energy wanes. Our enthusiasm ebbs away. Take the new family pet. Everyone loves the idea of getting a gerbil—initially, at least. The first week is full of fun and engagement, with all hands on deck. But then you are left with three years of cleaning out a cage and buying gerbil bedding and gerbil food. We have short attention spans. We lose interest in things. That is just how it is.

Abraham lived a long life and God made some big commitments to him and to his family, but the story moves slowly. It goes on for about a hundred years and for over ten chapters of the Bible, which is quite a lot for any one person. Abraham has his own ups and downs in following the Lord and serving him, and as we come now to the very end of Abraham's very long life, we might wonder if the Lord has retained interest in him, or whether he has moved on to a new bright young leader and to the next endeavor? This closing section of the Abraham story is a beautiful and vivid reminder of the persistent faithfulness of God, that he is good to his servants and to their children. It is a powerful reminder that he is committed to his plans and his promises, not just for the short term, but for the long run.

The focus in this closing section of the life story of Abraham is the search for a bride for Isaac. It is a lovely story. As we enjoy it, we need to remember again why it matters within the big picture of God's salvation plan. God had promised to make a great nation of Abraham, to bless him, to make him a blessing, and to bring blessing to the world through him. Isaac was born through the promises of God and by miraculous means. But for the family to continue, for the blessing to grow and the promises to be fulfilled, Isaac needs a family of his own. He needs to marry and have children. This matters because it is *this promise* to *this family* that leads straight through the history of Israel to the stable in Bethlehem, to the cross of Calvary, and to the gospel of our salvation. God does not lose interest in his project or his plan or his chosen family. He is persistent in his kindness and his blessings, and his persistence is meant to teach and shape us. That is exactly what happened in the life of Abraham.

The Lord teaches his servants through his blessings

I am sure you are familiar with the image of the stick and the carrot. If you want to get an obstinate donkey to move, there are essentially two strategies you can adopt. You can apply the stick to the rear of the donkey or dangle the carrot in front of its nose. Often both might be needed. Have you considered how it is that you learn best to trust and obey the Lord? Is it by warnings, chastisements, and acts of discipline—by the stick, as it were? Those things certainly have their place in the life of the believer, there is no question. But the God of the Bible so often teaches us using the carrot of his blessing. He patiently woos us to follow, trust, and obey him through the enticements of his kindness. He does it again and again. It matches his character as we see it in the gospel. He overwhelms us with his grace and generosity. That is just who he is.

That is certainly the way things worked in the life of Abraham. Notice what his experience had been: "Now Abraham was old, well advanced in years. And the LORD had blessed Abraham in all things" (24:1). What a wonderful thing to be able to record and report of a believer's life. The Lord had blessed Abraham in all things. That is not to say his life had been without complication or grief. He had had the challenge of leaving his homeland, the self-imposed heartache of seeing his wife taken into a forced marriage with Pharaoh of Egypt, the sadness of parting ways with his nephew Lot, the grief of sending his wife Hagar and son Ishmael into the wilderness. There were plenty of things in life that ended up being tough, many of which were due to his own folly. But there was no question that the Lord had blessed him richly and abundantly. The Lord had intervened and overcome Abraham and Sarah's folly, given them a son, prospered their work, and granted them material abundance. He had given them favor with the people of the land. The sheer kindness of God had taught Abraham something. It had taught him to trust God, it had taught him to obey God. It had taught him *faithfulness* in his walk with the Lord. Just notice how verse 2 follows on from verse 1:

> "the LORD had blessed Abraham in all things… And Abraham said to his servant, the oldest of his household, who had charge of all that he had, 'Put your hand under my thigh, that I may make you swear by the LORD, the God of heaven and God of the earth, that you will not take a wife for my son from the daughters of the Canaanites, among whom I dwell, but will go to my

> country and to my kindred, and take a wife for my son Isaac'" (24:1–4).

What is Abraham doing here? What is the significance? Remember who he is and who his family are. They have been set apart by the Lord to be his special people and recipients of his great promises, especially his salvation. They are distinct from the nations. They know and worship the Lord and belong to him. But Abraham and his son Isaac are living among Gentiles, among people who do not yet know the Lord. In a sense, they are pioneers in the Promised Land before it has been fully claimed. Abraham is now faced with concern for the family's future and especially about the matter of finding a wife for Isaac. In that day and age, this was primarily the father's responsibility, and Abraham feels the weight of it. The easy thing would be to go round the local families in the surrounding villages and towns to seek out a wife among the Hittites and the Canaanites. That way Abraham could get to know the family and meet the young lady. She and Isaac could perhaps get to know each other. It would be convenient and safe.

But Abraham will not do that. In fact, he binds his leading servant to swear to him with this intimate oath that he will not allow Isaac to marry a Canaanite, but rather that he will go back to Abraham's homeland to find a wife from among his kindred. The point here is very simple. Abraham wants Isaac to marry within the wider family of promise and not to go to the Gentiles. It is a principle that runs right through Scripture. The people of God are to marry from among the people of God. We see it reaffirmed in the New Testament: believers must not be unequally yoked with unbelievers (2 Corinthians 6:14). The believer must marry someone who belongs to the Lord (1 Corinthians 7:39). It is a consistent principle, and it makes sense. If the Lord is everything to his people and he calls us to a life set apart for him, it is going to be hard to pursue that life if our spouse does not share our devotion to the Lord.

It is clear and logical enough, but this can be one of the more stretching faith tests believers face. There is hardly a bigger life decision or more momentous life change than getting married. For many individual believers and their parents, this issue looms large. *Who will I marry? Will I find the right person? Will my son or daughter find the right person?* As the years go by and a sense of urgency rises, the question becomes more pressing: *Will I hold onto this basic criterion to marry within the family of God? Will I keep encouraging my son or daughter in that way? Or when the nice non-Christian—the charming Canaanite—comes along, will my principles shift?* I do not need to go far down this road for you to recognize that this is a huge issue for the family of God. It always has been. Maybe you just have not found a believer and do not see the prospect of one on the horizon. Maybe you are having to choose between singleness (which is perhaps not what you want) or marrying outside the faith, and you must ask the question: *Can I trust the Lord with this?* Or your son or daughter is in that place and, as a parent, you are watching, on the emotional rollercoaster with them, and wrestling with the question in your own heart: *Can I trust the Lord with this?*

Abraham is insistent. Maybe some years before he would have been pragmatic and gone for the easy option. But having walked with the Lord and having seen his incredible faithfulness over time, he now knows: *I can trust God with this and my responsibility is faithfulness.* Abraham must know that he might not live to see the outcome of all this. Nonetheless he wants his insistence honored and he calls his servant to make an oath that he will not have Isaac marry from among the Canaanites.

Abraham's servant raises a real issue: *What if the woman I find will not come here? Shall we take Isaac back to your homeland?*

His question is not an unnatural one, but Abraham refuses the obvious answer. He will not have the plan of God compromised by a retreat from the land of promise. Abraham says to his servant: *Do not take my son back there. God has brought me here. God has made a covenant with me about this land of promise.* And he explains:

> "The Lord, the God of heaven, who took me from my father's house and from the land of my kindred, and who spoke to me and swore to me, 'To your offspring I will give this land,' he will send his angel before you, and you shall take a wife for my son from there'" (verse 7).

The Lord will have this in hand, his angel will go before you. That is Abraham's confidence, a confidence he has learned over time. It is not what he said when he and Sarah went down to Egypt, and it is not what he said when they encountered King Abimelech, but it is what he says now.

God called us here to Canaan, says Abraham, *and if he does not provide the right wife for Isaac in his way, then we will have to just leave it, you are not bound*, "you will be free from this oath of mine" (24:8). *But we are not compromising on what God has said and what God has called us to do.* Now, that is faithfulness. That is trusting God enough to do what is right. Trusting him to do what you know is right, even when it looks risky and hard and costly and even unlikely. It is about a life that is given over to serving the Lord, obeying his Word, and doing his will.

You may remember that the first words recorded from Abraham in his story were the misleading words he gave to Sarah to speak to Pharaoh in Genesis 12. The words to his servant here in Genesis 24:2–8 are his final recorded words. They are words of faith in the covenant promises, words of integrity. What a contrast.[1] But the contrast is there because Abraham has learned over time and through experiencing the sheer blessing and kindness of God in such a way that he knew he could trust him. Abraham's faithfulness in 24:2 follows his experience in verse 1: "Now Abraham was old, well advanced in years. And the LORD had blessed him in all things." Abraham's experience and testimony call us to ask: Where is God calling us to a risky, unlikely, potentially costly, certainly uncomfortable *faithfulness*? Where is he calling you to do the right thing against the odds, by faith and not by sight—the right thing that is so much harder than the wrong thing? Maybe it is in this question of marriage. Will you trust God enough to do what is right and to wait on him for the outcome? Maybe it is some other big life decision. Maybe it is something relatively smaller. As you consider that, let me encourage you to learn from the faithfulness of God. Look back and see how he has blessed you in every way. See how good he has been to you and trust him for what lies ahead. Trust him with your costly acts of faithfulness.

God persists in blessing his servants to the end

The way this story proceeds is just pure delight. It is a little dream-like and quite lovely—and it speaks volumes of the heart and character of God. The servant of Abraham loads up ten camels with choice gifts from his master (24:10). This is an impressive delegation from a rich man's house. This is ten gleaming Range Rovers with the trunks stuffed full of packages and gifts from the finest retailers: boxes from Tiffany's and Nordstrom, Selfridges and Bloomingdale's, Gucci and Prada. And off they go.

When they arrive, this servant—who is clearly a godly person of real faith—kneels by the well and prays a wonderful prayer. It is the first substantial personal petition in the Bible:

> "O LORD, God of my master Abraham, please grant me success today and show steadfast love to my master

> Abraham. Behold, I am standing by the spring of water, and the daughters of the men of the city are coming out to draw water" (24:12–13).

He asks that the young woman who comes willing to help draw water might be the right one.

It is a good prayer for guidance and a lovely prayer of faith. Before he was done speaking, the Lord brought the answer (24:15). Rebekah, a beautiful maiden, was the woman of God's choosing (24:16). She shows herself kind and hospitable and she helps these travelers at the well. Abraham's servant asks for help with watering the camels and she kindly obliges. This is not a small favor. There are ten camels, and each could have lost 25 gallons of water in a journey such as theirs.[2] Drawing 250 gallons of water is not a small favor at all, but Rebekah proves herself gracious and industrious. She only rises in our estimation. The servant asks if there might be room at her father's house for these travelers and she insists that there is, along with straw and fodder for the camels. This servant can see the Lord's hand in all this, and his heart overflows:

> "The man bowed his head and worshipped the Lord and said, 'Blessed be the Lord, the God of my master Abraham, who has not forsaken his steadfast love and his faithfulness toward my master. As for me, the Lord has led me in the way to the house of my master's kinsmen'" (verses 26–27).

Rebekah runs home to say what has happened and her brother Laban comes out and invites the servant in. He tells the household the whole story, and then Laban and Rebekah's father Bethuel respond:

> "The thing has come from the LORD; we cannot speak to you bad or good. Behold, Rebekah is before you; take her and go, and let her be the wife of your master's son, as the LORD has spoken" (verses 50–51).

They do, however, suggest a delay to allow the thing to settle. But Abraham's servant feels an urgency to get back to his master, and so they ask Rebekah, "Will you go with this man?" (24:58). We can hardly imagine what kind of thoughts and questions must have been turning over in her mind, but she replies simply, in a way that the Lord himself must have enabled: "I will go" (24:58). She is willing and she departs with the blessing of her family. It is all so astounding, so unlikely, so God-ordained. What are the odds of finding a young woman, of the right family, of the right heart, at the right place, at the right time, who is both kind and beautiful? No one could have planned this out. Abraham certainly could not have orchestrated it. But the Lord did it. Laban and Bethuel were right: "The thing has come from the LORD" (24:50).

Of course, the all-important thing has not yet happened. Isaac and Rebekah have not met. Perhaps this is the most delightful part of the story. As the entourage returns, Isaac is out in the fields meditating and is spending time with the Lord (24:63). He looks up, and camels are coming: "And Rebekah lifted up her eyes, and when she saw Isaac, she dismounted from the camel" (24:64). She asks the servant, "Who is that man?" (24:65)—that man whose eyes have met hers. She discovers it is Isaac. The servant tells Isaac the grand story. "Then Isaac brought her into the tent of Sarah his mother and took Rebekah, and she became his wife, and he loved her" (24:67). It is, quite literally, a marriage made in heaven. It is a beautiful thing, a lovely story.

It is certainly a heart-warming account. But what are we to see in it? What are we meant to learn? On one level, we see here that God is not in the business of planning meagre gifts and minor blessings for those who trust him and follow him. God is bountifully generous and wonderfully kind, and his plans are good plans, *really good plans*. That is not to say that everyone who wants to get married will find the person of their dreams and that it will end with misty eyes meeting across a sun-dappled field and love at first sight. That is not the point. The point is that God is able to guide. He is able to provide. He is able to do more than we anticipate or expect. He is faithful to those who entrust themselves to him, faithful to his servants, and good to his children.

Abraham has been following the Lord for something approaching a hundred years at this point. There have been ups and downs, but the Lord has not wavered. He has not given up, he has not changed course and he has not lost interest. He has not lost interest in Abraham or Abraham's family, *and he has not lost interest in his greater plan*. That is the point of ultimate significance here.

There are certain kinds of projects that stretch beyond the working life of any of the participants in the work—the Great Wall of China, a major city's subway system, the cathedrals of the medieval world. These projects stretched for decades, sometimes centuries. The Great Wall of China was completed over two millennia. England's York Minster Cathedral took 252 years to build. In some cases, despite a master plan at the beginning, there is a sense in which the work is never done. The great danger with a project like that is that the key players will lose interest or resources or the opportunity to continue the work beyond the day of its founders. None of the principal architects will be around long enough to see the work through.

The great comfort here in this passage is the assurance that God himself is committed to his people. He is committed to his covenant family, his plan, and his great blessing. Abraham is not going to be around to see the job completed. And yet, before his death, the Lord shows Abraham his persistence in blessing and his commitment to finishing the work. Abraham is allowed to die in the knowledge that there is provision for the family and that the next stage of the plan is in hand. He dies at the good old age of 175 years, is gathered to his people, and buried alongside Sarah in the cave he bought for her, in the Promised Land (25:7–10). But the story of God's work does not stop with his death, and the blessing of God upon his people does not cease: "After the death of Abraham, God blessed Isaac his son. And Isaac settled at Beer-lahai-roi" (25:11).

One of the issues of faith we will all grapple with in some measure is this: *How is the work of the gospel in my church or family, in the ministry I am involved in, or in society more broadly, going to go forward after my day?* Maybe you have had a significant ministry role, or built some gospel outreach, or been the "spiritual glue" in your wider family, or supported gospel ministry financially in a significant way. *How will it look when I am no longer able to give, or teach, or lead, or serve? The cathedral is half built, and I am not going to live to see it finished.* Genesis 25 is such an encouragement. God is persistent. He is tenacious and unyielding in pouring out his blessing on his people and furthering his plan and his work. You will have to stop eventually. You will have to hand over the reins. But God has got the bigger picture in view, and he cares more about the work than you do. He loves the people involved even more than you love them, and he will not give up or forget.

The family story that moves forward through the gift of a wife for Isaac continues through the whole Old Testament. It points to the coming of a child—a many-times great-grandchild of Isaac and Rebekah—who would arrive according to the plan of God, and who would live and die and rise again to fulfill God's promises of blessing to the world through the forgiveness of sin. The story points forward to his return and to a future in a greater land above for the entire family of faith. Abraham needed to see God's persistence in giving his blessings, and we need to register it too.

The death of great servants of God is always hard for the people of God. The Victorian preacher Charles Spurgeon spoke to congregations of thousands and was beloved in Britain and beyond. With his untimely death in his 50s, I am sure that many felt that the evangelical movement must run out of steam. After all, how could the church go on without him? Or, more recently, we might think of the death of evangelist Billy Graham who in so many ways embodied and personified the evangelical movement in the English-speaking world. We might ask who could possibly take up his role and move things forward, but the answer is simple: God is moving things forward. He will make provision for his people, for his church, and for his plan. The gospel will continue to go out. New leaders will be raised up. The Spirit will be given to those who believe. The Lord Jesus will come back. The church will be built and the very gates of hell will not prevail against it. God is persistent and unyielding in bestowing his blessing.

Conclusion

The story of Abraham is first and foremost the story of God's saving grace, announced to Abraham, seen in his life, and fulfilled in the person and work of the Lord Jesus Christ. Here in this story we have the gospel declared and the gospel displayed. God announces his promises to Abraham for his family and for the wider world. Lest we imagine that Abraham is a special kind of hero deserving of this privilege, we are soon disabused of this notion. He is shown to be feeble and frail, stumbling and sinful. And yet the Lord gives him privilege after privilege, and he works out his purposes through him.

Watching the life of Abraham unfold points us again and again to the God of astounding grace—and it gives us wonderful hope that the Lord can and will save and use ordinary and frail people. Even people like us. For us, as the children of God, what a privilege it is to know this God as our gracious and faithful Father, to learn faithfulness through his kindness, and to have the assurance of his commitment to bless and to keep us to the end.

However, it is possible that you have read through this study without feeling any of this assurance because you do not know this God personally. You may be thinking that there is something attractive in the story of Abraham's life because of the assurance and security he enjoyed in the grace of God. But you know that you do not have what he had. If that is the case for you, please know that there is room for you in the family of God. This God of persistent blessing welcomes all into his family who will enter through faith in his Son. The Lord Jesus Christ, great Abraham's greater son, died so that you might be cleansed of sin, forgiven, welcomed in. He died so that you might have the security and purpose and hope that belonged to Abraham and to Isaac and to all the children of God. Would you respond to that invitation, even today?

Endnotes

Chapter 2

1 Duguid perceptively identifies the test here as "the test of prosperity." Ian M. Duguid, *Living in the Gap Between Promise and Reality* (P&R Publishing, 2015), pp. 29–30.

2 I was helped by Duguid's observation that Lot's materialism and Abraham's open-handed approach were at the heart of the issue in this chapter. Duguid, *Living in the Gap*, pp. 27–38.

3 See Duguid, *Living in the Gap*, p. 34.

4 Quoted in Gordon J. Wenham, *Word Biblical Commentary: Genesis 1–15* (Word Books, 1987), p. 298, whose insightful treatment of the geographical notes in this section (pp. 297–298) was beneficial here.

5 Lucy Warwick-Ching, "Inheritance disputes rise as families go to war over estates," *Financial Times*, July 16, 2020.

6 See Duguid, *Living in the Gap*, p. 36.

Chapter 3

1 Duguid similarly and rightly identifies here a picture of the work of Jesus Christ that stands behind and before any model for our own behavior and response. Duguid, *Living in the Gap*, p. 43.

2 Chris Martin and Nic Querolo, "A $1 billion solar plant was obsolete before it ever went online," *Bloomberg.com*, January 6, 2020.

Chapter 4

1 Duguid helpfully draws out the emotional and spiritual dynamics of Abraham's temptation to fear at this point in the narrative. Duguid, *Living in the Gap*, pp. 51–55.

2 Romans 4:19–20 affirms to us that Abraham did not slide into fearful unbelief, even if the Lord's admonition and Abraham's response here indicate that he was at the very least tempted to fear. The comments of Tom Schreiner on Romans 4:19–20 are insightful: "How can Paul make this statement when the Genesis narrative (Gen. 12–24) obviously includes regressions as well as advances in Abraham's faith? The answer is that Paul is not trying to chronicle in detail the ups and downs of faith in the life of Abraham. The words 'he did not doubt'... characterize the basic pattern and direction of Abraham's life, which was ultimately typified by trust in God, not by doubt. He didn't waver in the sense that he persevered and persisted in faith." Thomas R. Schreiner, Romans (Baker Academic, 2018), p. 245.

3 John D. Currid, *Genesis* vol. 1 (Evangelical Press, 2015), p. 295.

4 Tom Mullen, "The man who survive eight Nazi death camps," *BBC News Online*, October 5, 2015.

5 I appreciated and benefitted from the way in which Duguid shows how this incident points us forward to the cross of Christ. Duguid, *Living in the Gap*, pp. 58–61.

Chapter 6

1 Forrester Research, in Sharon Markovsky, "In the Age of the Consumer, Engagement is King!" Sharon Markovsky's Practical Discussions of Marketing, July 12, 2011, https://sharonmarkovsky.wordpress.com/2011/07/12/welcome-to-the-age-of-the-consumer/

2 Allen P. Ross, Creation and Blessing (Baker Academic, 1998), p. 332.

Chapter 8

1 Although I have not been able to locate the original source of this oft-repeated observation, I believe it traces back to Gordon Dahl.

2 I am indebted to Mark Ashton, my former pastor in Cambridge, for this illustration.

Chapter 9

1 Currid highlights this truth in his treatment of this passage, commenting that "Each of us has a deeply worn channel of a corrupt nature—besetting sins that refuse to let us go. And these sins come in cycles. They revisit us time and time again." Currid, *Genesis* vol. 1, p. 370.

Chapter 12

1 Duguid insightfully highlights the way in which Abraham's understanding of himself as an "alien and stranger" in the world shapes his behavior in this chapter, not least by helping him to loosen his grip on the things of this world. These insights helped give shape to the exegesis that follows here. Duguid, *Living in the Gap*, pp. 152–157.

Chapter 13

1 Currid, *Genesis* vol. 1, p. 415.

2 Currid, *Genesis* vol. 1.

Scripture Index

Jude

Revelation

Acknowledgements

This study of the Abraham narrative took shape initially in the pulpit of the Metropolitan Bible Church in Ottawa, Canada, where I have the privilege of serving. I often say to other pastors and to those training for ministry that it is ideal to serve in a church that loves preaching, because the congregation will draw the preaching out of the preacher by their appetite for the Word of God. That has been my happy experience, and I believe that this study of Abraham has been enriched by the interest and appetite of the church family to hear and receive this portion of God's revealed Word. I am thankful to our elders for their continued encouragement to write. I doubt very much that this project would have been possible without that kind and ongoing encouragement.

Jonathan Pountney and the wider editorial team at Evangelical Press have been wonderful partners in shaping this project and bringing it to fruition, and I am grateful to them. As ever, the work of producing a book takes time and attention, and I am aware that this always involves an irreducible degree of sacrifice on the part of my wife, Gemma, and our children. They are more gracious and forbearing than I deserve, and I am thankful to them and for them.

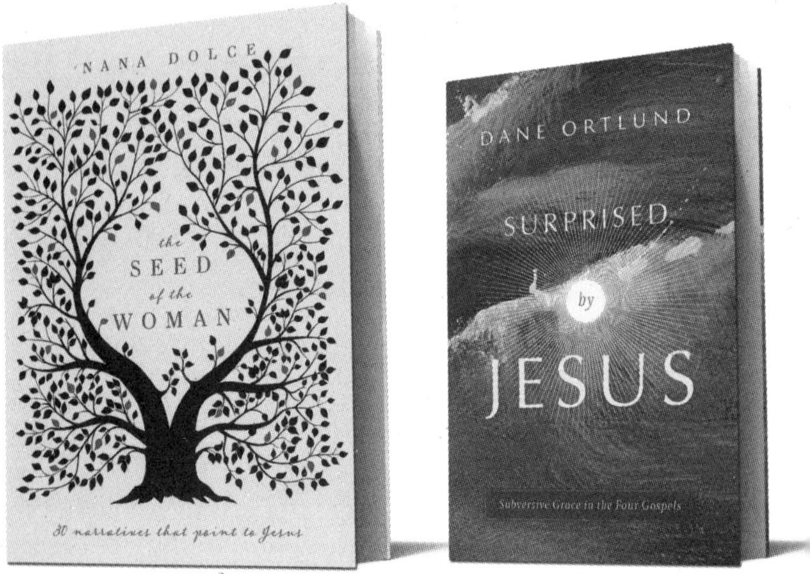
NANA DOLCE
the SEED of the WOMAN
30 narratives that point to Jesus
DANE ORTLUND
SURPRISED by JESUS
Subversive Grace in the Four Gospels